SHE FOUND **HER**
SUPERPOWER

7 Women

7 Divorces

7 Strengths Unlocked

SHE

7 WOMEN

FOUND

7 DIVORCES

HER

7 STRENGTHS UNLOCKED

SUPERPOWER

**Audrey Alice, Lauren Baca, Kathryn Bisland,
Olga Dewar, Michelle Wincell O'Leary,
Nathalie Perron, and Deepika Sandhu**

ISBN 978-1-968944-03-2 *(paperback)*
ISBN 978-1-968944-04-9 *(kindle)*

CONTENTS

INTRODUCTION

By Deepika Sandhu

"She doesn't know it yet."

I found myself smiling, a little too big. A smile that says I know something you don't know. Which in that moment, I did. But the look didn't match the situation. I should have been serious. If not serious, at least empathetic. Certainly not smiling, almost smirking. But I couldn't help it. My entire self—my mind, my spirit and my face—was reacting to what I knew would eventually unlock for her: a superpower. But she had no idea.

All she knew was the abuse. The financial manipulation, the heartache she was experiencing.

But I could see so much more.

My friend asked me to meet her.

"She read your book and really wants to talk to you. She is
going through a divorce."

This happened to me countless times. Friends, family,
readers I had never met before wanting to share their
relationship and divorce journeys with me. I always listened.
A faltering relationship. A divorce. Rebuilding a new life.
Everything I too endured. All of it can be so isolating. It
certainly was for me. So if I could lend an ear, support in
some way, I always did.

But this time hit different.

We met at a cute cafe about an equal distance from each
other's homes. She had beautiful wavy locks, striking
eyes and an outfit perfect for the summer day. She looked
effortlessly chic on the outside. But on the inside, she
was spinning in a constant cycle of replaying moments in
her marriage. Trying to make sense of every fight, every
misunderstanding, or outright deceit that played out inside
her home. Seeking to explain them, minimize them, and
incessantly searching for any reason, however tiny, to
stay in the marriage.

As we sipped our coffee, a cappuccino for me and a matcha
for her, she recounted detail after detail of her failing
marriage. The time they got in a shouting match while
driving in a snow storm. All the times he left her at home
alone while he went to party with his friends. The close
"friendships" he was forming with other women. The way
he gaslit her into handing him her money from before

marriage so he could invest it "properly" with no record, no evidence, and no access to see how it was used.

At the end of each memory she repeated the same few lines.

I don't want to ruin my life.

My parents won't be able to handle this.

What will people say?

Maybe it isn't as bad as I think.

Maybe I am the one being dramatic.

My kids will resent me for leaving.

That's when I smiled, a big, warm, all-knowing smile.

She seemed a little shocked, likely wondering why this lady has the nerve to smile at her terrible story.

I knew she was afraid. I knew she was stuck. I knew she bravely came to meet me seeking inspiration, insight and help. But I couldn't help myself.

She didn't know it yet, but all these stories she was telling herself were about to become her strongest superpowers. How did I know? They were once my story too. Every single one.

Going through my divorce, every possible terrifying thought of how my life would unfold if I wasn't married showed its face:

My life will end. No one else will want me! Do I think I can do better? What about money? Will I lose all the money I worked so hard for? The cost of this divorce will bankrupt me! My poor kid. I don't want her to grow up in a broken home. Oh, and my personal favorite: *What would people say?*

But guess what? None of those stories showed up in my reality.

Why?

Because I decided to morph every one of those false narratives into a superpower.

Just like Wonder Woman spins rapidly to change into her superhero costume, I too spun up those old beliefs and created new ones. Instead of thinking my life would be ruined, I decided to believe that I would step into a life that would feel right on all fronts. And I did.

Instead of being fixated on what people would say about me and my divorce, I decided to believe that I would create new, meaningful and more aligned connections. And I did.

Instead of believing that I was being dramatic or convincing myself my marriage wasn't as bad as it felt, I decided to believe that how I felt mattered, how I wished to experience this life mattered and that I could move towards a life that felt amazing each and every day in small meaningful ways. And I did.

Instead of believing no one else would come along to love me, I decided to believe that truly learning to love myself was the road to fully receiving the love of others. So I did.

Instead of believing I was ruining my kid's life by divorcing, I decided to believe that having two parents, happy in their respective homes, was far better than a sad, disconnected, and unloving group of people living under one roof. I decided to believe that if my daughter could see her mom thriving on all fronts, that she too would know to expect nothing less from her own life. And this is exactly what was happening for me.

This is what I want for you too.

Even if you can't see how it can happen for you.

Even if you can't see the path.

Even if today feels too heavy and hard, can you lean into believing that all of this is happening for you?

Can you believe that something better will unlock?

Can you believe that your superpower will be shown?

Can you believe that you will step into a new version of your story, one that feels like the version you were always meant to live?

I think you can.

The stories in this book are here to show you exactly that. For each of the women sharing their story, what seemed like the end turned out to be the most beautiful beginning. Divorcing wasn't a death sentence or a declaration of eternal sorrow, but instead a key to unlocking their own superpowers that helped them create lives they now love.

And it will be for you too.

Deepika

Deepika is the CEO of Soul Sparks Press, a six-time award-winning, bestselling author, TV show host, and recently retired Silicon Valley Business Executive. Deepika Sandhu created Soul Sparks Press, a bespoke publishing house with soul, to combine the polish of traditional publishing with the empowerment of self-publishing, ensuring authors retain ownership, royalties, and collaborative creativity over their books. With more than 80 signed authors, Soul Sparks Press is redefining what it means to share a story, offering coaching, editing, design, publishing, and launch support in a nurturing, community-driven environment.

Deepika lives in the San Francisco Bay Area with her sweet and sassy pre-teen daughter and their puppy.

Connect with Deepika on instagram @deepikasandhu.co or at Soul Sparks Press soulsparkspress.com

⚡

1

THE DRESS
I COULDN'T
LET GO OF

By Natalie Perron

FOR NATHALIE FROM THE FIELD OF LOVE

"By staying, I enabled him to be stuck
By leaving, I enabled him to be free.
If he's not ready, that's not my fault.
While he feels the pain of contraction;
I experience the Gift of expansion
The guilt lives in my EGO
I live in the Brilliance."

WRITTEN BY NANCY REGAN
HALIFAX, NOVA SCOTIA, CANADA

Nothing like a flood to remind you of items that have been tucked away for safe keeping. As I cleaned up the basement of our home, sorting and purging, I came across many items that tugged at my heartstrings, but none more than the pretty box containing my wedding dress.

It had survived the flood and was still in immaculate condition, twenty-seven years after my wedding day and eleven years since my divorce. Why was I still keeping it? I told myself that I was saving it for my daughter, but she'd already told me she didn't want it. The real reason, I knew, was much more complicated. Seeing it again was like a slap, a reminder of the story I had told myself about how I'd failed my husband and my children.

I knew that in order to fully move on, I needed to let this dress, and this story, go. But I felt well and truly stuck. I knew I couldn't just throw it away; it felt important for the dress to be reused for something meaningful. I went looking on the internet, and I reached out to people with no response.

Over a period of years, I would move the box with my wedding dress in it from place to place in my home, each time feeling a unique combination of sadness, shame, and powerlessness. Finally, after sharing my difficulty letting go with a group I was taking part in, and receiving some support and accountability, I took a baby step and moved my wedding dress from the house to the backseat of the car.

And now here I am sitting in the car in front of the consignment store, willing myself to go in. My hands are sweating, and I feel the slow spread of shame in my chest. I look into the backseat, to the fancy box that I was once so proud of. My wedding dress. I force myself out of the car and into the crisp fall air, retrieving the box and gently carrying it into the store.

I feel a shiver from the cold wind as I walk. It's a dull, sunless sky kind of day. I quietly say to myself, "I can do hard things. I know letting go is the right thing to do for my growth, to make space within for new experiences."

The bell above the door jangles, but no one comes. The store smells stuffy and, as I take a few tentative steps in, I notice a clerk behind the counter. She's on her phone and, as I approach, she seems to be trying to finish a text or a game before turning her face up to look at me. She doesn't smile. I immediately take this to be a bad sign, a sign that I'm doing something wrong, a sign that I shouldn't be trying to get rid of this sacred part of my past.

"Do you accept wedding dresses?" I ask, my voice shaking.

"Depends," she answers, looking at the box in my arms. "How old is it?"

"Twenty-seven years old," I say, feeling my face flush.

The clerk starts to shake her head before she even answers. "We don't accept anything that old," she says. "Only one or two years." She looks disappointed in me.

I feel stunned and ill-prepared for this response. I hear myself thanking her in a monotone voice and slowly turn around, with my head down. Tears quietly run down my cheeks as I make my way to the door.

At the car, I put my dress in the back seat again and close the door. I sit and stare straight ahead, wondering why this was happening and if it's a sign I'm supposed to keep it, a sign perhaps that I never should have left my husband.

. . .

I stand at the living room window of my family home, my body pressed against the cold pane, my stomach in knots. He was supposed to be here thirty minutes ago, our special holiday dinner is ready, and all my family is waiting.

"Don't worry," my mother had said moments ago, stroking my arm. "He's just taking it easy in this weather. He'll be here in no time." New Brunswick winters are never easy, but this storm seems especially brutal and frightening. I hope nothing serious has happened to him. I wonder if he should even be attempting to drive up since he works so far away.

I try to let my mother's words reassure me as the rich fragrance of her special beef bourguignon—that wonderful blend of herbs, red wine, onions, and mushrooms—reaches me in the living room. Peering out in swirling snow, I can feel the wind rattling the window and I can't even see the road from the house.

He is never late, and it had been that way right from the beginning of our relationship seven years ago, when I was just fifteen. He is careful and considerate and always puts me first. He's the kind of person who walks on the roadside when we're on the sidewalk together. Always protecting me.

Suddenly, I see a flash of red coming up the long driveway. "He's here!" I shout to my family and run to the front door. Snow blows into the foyer as I stand with the door open, my heart beating wildly.

He is just getting out of his car, a bag in one hand and what looks like flowers in the other. By the time he gets to the porch, his coat and hair are white with flakes, but oh, that smile. The one he reserves only for me.

Tears spring to my eyes, and I launch myself into his arms before he can even get in the door. "I was so worried," I cried. "I'm so glad you're here."

We head into the kitchen together, where the dining table is carefully curated with mom's dinnerware and cutlery—the ones we only use for special meals. After everyone greets him, we sit down side-by-side, and I take a deep breath, relieved that he is here and that both of our families have come together.

There are ten of us around the table, his parents, my parents, my two sisters, and my grandparents. A special day indeed. He and I hold hands as my Mom prepares and serves each guest. I can feel something electric coming from him as he fidgets in his chair next to me, and keeps turning to shyly smile at me.

My Mom prepares and serves each guest a dinner plate as my father opens a bottle of wine. The candles flicker, and with a pretend waiter flair, my dad carefully and slowly fills each glass allowing the wine to dance in the glass with each pour.

After his father says a prayer of thanks and my father toasts the chef, we clink our glasses together and drink. The electric hum beside me reaches a crescendo as he gets up from his chair. He looks at me with a nervous smile and clears his throat. What is going on, I wonder?

Suddenly, he drops to one knee beside me, and all becomes crystal clear. I am in disbelief at the same time that this moment feels absolutely right. "I am in love with you, Nathalie. I have been since the moment I met you," he says gently, looking deep into my eyes.

Butterflies dance in my stomach and tears prick my eyes. I feel a gentle swell of emotion surround us as a burgundy wooden ring box appears in his hands. He opens the lid, revealing a beautiful diamond ring. "I'd love it if you'd be my wife?"

My heart feels close to bursting as I murmur "Yes," and he carefully places the ring on my finger. The room erupts in clapping and cheering as we kiss and hug each other.

My father gets up off his chair and makes his way over, shaking his hand. "Congratulations," he says. "I know you are going to take good care of my daughter."

At this moment, I am happier than I have ever been, and my father's blessing is the icing on the cake. It means the world to me.

. . .

Out of all the preparation that went into planning our fairy tale wedding, the choosing and purchasing of my wedding dress had the most meaning. I truly felt like the dress chose me. I loved the heart shaped neckline, the smooth, soft and luxurious satin, and the way it made me feel beautiful—like a queen.

When I look back at that young woman who bought her dress from the best dress shop in town, I see someone who believed she needed a man in her life. My upbringing had taught me to choose a husband who would always take care of me. I believed we were going to build a life together and do all the things we loved until it was time to retire. I truly believed with every ounce of my being that we would live a long and happy life together. There was no other option to entertain.

But life had other plans.

After five years of marriage, I was at work just finishing up my day when I got a phone call that would change my life. It was my husband telling me he had broken his ankle and was heading to the hospital. This simple injury ended in him experiencing a double pulmonary embolism that no one expected. Overnight, his behavior toward me changed, and it would be a few years before there was any explanation of what had happened.

. . •

It is early morning about six months after his incident and I am awakened by him shaking me frantically.

I have the sense that he has been talking to me for awhile and trying to wake me. His voice is hoarse and anxious. "Can you call my work and tell them I can't come in today?"

"What?" I ask, leaning up and reaching for my eyeglasses on the night table.

"I'm sick and I need you to call my work and tell them I can't come in." He is peering at me in the early morning light, fidgeting with the covers.

"Why can't you call?" I feel groggy and confused and a little bit worried. My husband loved his work and before his injury had never missed a day. This is highly unusual. I sit up in bed to better deal with whatever was happening.

"You need to call!" He leaps up and starts pacing beside our bed.

"What's going on? If you're sick, you need to call yourself. I can't do that for you." I feel my heart start to beat faster, my stomach begins to clench.

This isn't the first strange thing to happen in the last few months. He'd been forgetting to do things he used to pride himself on: paying our bills on time and remembering our anniversary. He'd also begun losing patience over small things that he wouldn't have even blinked at before. Throwing a bicycle across the lawn when he couldn't figure out how to put it on a bike rack. Pitching a piece of wood, and making a hole in the wall, when he couldn't figure out how to use the saw.

He storms over to my side of the bed, his face red and rigid, his fists squeezed into tight balls. "Pick up the phone and call!" he screams. It must have been the look on my face that caused him to come to his senses and back away. I had become terrified of my husband.

. . .

Over the next few years, I tried to make it work—we even had two children together—but faced with multiple other traumatic life events, including the death of my father at the young age of fifty-six, and the birth of a son with disabilities all while studying to get my Masters in Social Work, a new requirement for my employment. I felt myself crumbling.

It took several years to discover that his enormous behavior changes were a result of the event of impairment. Knowing this was helpful, but it didn't make it any easier. In essence, I was married to a stranger, and over time it began to take a huge toll.

I felt trapped and no longer connected to my body. Chaos reigned, especially in my mind. I even developed a condition called trichotillomania (a hair-pulling disorder). Feeling anxious and paralyzed, I would find myself pulling out the hair of my eyebrows. When I noticed what I was doing, I would rush to the nearest mirror to see how much damage I had caused. For years, I had to carry an eyebrow liner to cover up what I was doing to myself.

I felt lost, with no compass to tell me which way to go. He had been my rock; my protector, my person. Who was I without his leadership? I was scared, hurt, exhausted, grieving, and depressed. My life was falling apart, and I wanted to run away from the situation. My deepest longings of that time were to recover my sense of self and to provide a place of peace, quiet, and calm for my beautiful children.

Then finally the day arrived when I simply couldn't do it anymore. I reached out to my husband's family to convey my desperation and ask for their help.

His family had always been supportive and were always there to lend us a hand. This time was no exception. When I explained how increasingly difficult the situation had become, how much he had changed, how frightened I was, they completely understood and stepped in to help me and our children. It was decided that he would stay at his sister's place and that they would support him during our separation. Knowing that he had his family to fall back on, and at a real breaking point myself, I chose a day when my mother was visiting our son in the living room and our daughter was at school. I asked my husband if we could talk downstairs in our home office.

"Why?" he asks, looking confused.

"I need to talk to you privately," I say, hearing my own voice catching in my throat.

We made our way down the staircase, and he sat in the black leather office chair. I could see that he had no idea what was coming, no idea I was about to ask for a separation, no idea that I was going to ask him to leave our home.

I stood just a few feet away from him, shaking inside, struggling to find my words, and feeling like my heart was going to jump out of my chest.

"I need some time by myself. I need to figure out what's next in our relationship." My voice was barely a whisper. There was a part of me, watching as an onlooker would, who couldn't believe that our marriage had come to this.

"What?" he says, the color draining from his face. I could see that he did not understand, would possibly never understand.

"You're not the same person. I feel like I don't know you anymore. You scare me with your outbursts." I force all of this out, knowing I need to get it out, and tell the truth. My truth. "You're not the man I married, and I can't feel our connection anymore. We're like roommates."

He stared at me, not moving.

"Your sister has agreed for you to go live with her for a little while. This time of separation will give us both the opportunity to decide what we want moving forward."

His face crumpled. "Nathalie, please don't do this," he pleaded. My heart broke.

An hour later, I stood at the picture window of our home and watched him put a suitcase into his sister's car. He took one last look at the house and stepped into the passenger side. I watched the car pull away, tears running down my face.

. . .

I spent a long time in a state of disbelief that in order to save myself and have some semblance of a life again, I had to force a separation. It was, by far, the hardest thing I ever had to do, and for a long time, there was no sense of joy or celebration on the other side. No relief or solace.

Instead, I felt terribly guilty and full of shame that I had not stood by my husband. That I literally could not survive. That I could not make it work.

Over time, some lightness prevailed. Family outings and visits with friends felt a bit lighter and easier, and in general, there was more ease in our home. I felt like a happier mother, but I also missed the man I had married tremendously. It felt like he had been snatched from us prematurely, and I experienced such anger for failing him, for failing us. I missed his presence, the good times, his laugh, and his kind and caring heart. And I deeply grieved both my husband and the father of my children.

· · ·

It's a late morning in December, a few months after our separation, and I am home in my bed lying under the covers, trembling and shivering out of control. It feels like I have a fever and there is a terrible pain in my abdomen area. I know something is wrong and I call my sister-in-law, who is a nurse, for advice.

She tries to sound calm, but I can tell she's rattled. "I am coming to get you and we're going to the emergency room," she says.

"But what about the kids?" I ask.

"Don't worry about them. I'll arrange for someone to come over." A feeling of relief passes through me, knowing someone else is in charge for a change.

By the time we get to the hospital, I feel sick to my stomach, and it's while the triage nurse is taking my vitals that I have to run to the nearest garbage can to vomit. They quickly admit me and from then on, I am in and out of consciousness. At various times, I'm aware of doctors and nurses talking over me, inserting catheters, taking blood, and hooking me up to IV fluids and medications.

I won't find out until later that I had been diagnosed with Toxic Shock Syndrome and was fighting for my life with multiple organs failing. My body was in rapid and severe shock, my family had been called, and the medical emergency team wasn't sure they were going to be able to save me.

. . .

Turns out that almost dying was the thing that ultimately began to save me, to awaken me. This episode shook me to my core and I was immensely grateful to be alive. When I look back, I see this illness as a blessing that opened up a healing portal. I realized that for many years I had been in strictly survival mode. I wasn't living, I wasn't enjoying life. I wasn't thriving. I no longer knew what my dreams were or what my heart wanted.

I decided it was time to get to know myself again and find out who I was, outside the history my husband and I had built together. The reality was that I'd been with him since I was fifteen years old, just an adolescent. I had built my identity around him.

When I met my husband, I found a safe place in him. He provided me with a life path. He was my protector. But the truth was that I didn't know who I was or how to love myself. When our life didn't turn out the way I'd longed for and planned, there were so many hopes, dreams, and expectations that were left unfulfilled.

Luckily for me, I had friends who initiated me to the concept of looking within for answers and who introduced me to spiritual leaders, guides, and mentors. One of these was the author Anne Bérubé. I attended her sessions, became a faithful student, and participated in retreats she offered. Within her community, I met incredible souls who became friends, but best of all I went on a self-discovery journey, and it has been the best gift I could ever have given myself. A life-affirming gift.

As I slowly rediscovered myself, I learned to use my voice, to heal, to release what I no longer needed, and to follow my intuition and my heart. This led me to an epiphany in my work life where I finally made good on a long-held dream—owning my own business. My son was in his mid teens and I knew that due to his disabilities, he could face a scarcity of employment opportunities as he grew into adulthood. I decided to approach my friends, who also have a son with challenges, and pitch a business idea. "Let's open a coffee shop and employ our children," I said. They agreed and today, I am a proud co-owner of a beautiful coffee shop called Cafe Inclusio. We have ten employees with intellectual and developmental disabilities and a community of volunteers that promote our motto: "A world of inclusion cup by cup."

As I healed my heart, I also met a beautiful man and opened myself to feel love again. To give myself permission to create new dreams and to be in a relationship again—with acquired wisdom and new beliefs this time around.

With courage and faith I build a new life, and I am proud of the woman I have become since the divorce. My self-discovery journey continues, and as I heal, more of who I truly am is revealed. I am still discovering new desires and uncovering new potential. I have also become aware of well-hidden wounds. Even though it had been fifteen years since the separation, and even though I had done what I needed to recover myself, I realized I was still wracked with tremendous guilt and shame for ending our marriage.

This awareness was a huge nugget that led to the writing of this chapter. "The cave you fear to enter holds the treasure you seek," said Joseph Campbell. It turns out that my cage was my divorce. I had to enter, shine a light on the darkness, and do something I never thought I'd be able to do—finally part with the one representation of my marriage that I had previously thought I could never part with. My wedding dress.

A proud mother of two, Nathalie Perron is a grounded visionary and seasoned Social Worker with over thirty-five years of experience in guiding others with compassion, wisdom, and leadership. A creative mystic at heart and a great friend to many, she finds joy in adventure, time in nature, and playing with mixed media—crafting her own journals and savoring the ritual of Inclusio signature coffee. As an entrepreneur and manifester, she blends art, purpose, and soulful living into everything she does. Rooted in New Brunswick, Canada, she continues to love life deeply—listening, creating, and living each day with presence and bliss.

2

A RETURN
TO LOVE

By Audrey Alice

Here I am, eight months pregnant, walking through the snow at 4 a.m. to get his drunk ass from the club.

Another day, another broken promise.

Another "I'll just go for one" that turned into me waking up at 4 a.m. to an empty bed and my heart pounding.

Where is he? My mind began to race, going straight to the worst case scenario.

I picked up my phone to call him.

No answer.

I dialed him again.

No answer.

I kept dialing while deciding whether or not to go get him.

Still no answer.

I got dressed, and checked on the kids. Fast asleep.

I watched their peaceful sleeping faces and their little chests rising and falling, and with each breath, I felt my throat tighten and the tears rise.

What have I done? Who have I chosen to have children with, and what example is this showing them?

That is when the anger kicked in.
I'm so sick of this shit. I should just leave you there and see what happens.

That seven-minute walk to the hotel nightclub at 4:30 a.m. in the middle of that freezing winter felt like the longest, coldest walk ever. As I entered the nightclub, where he had been overseeing an event he'd helped coordinate, all eyes turned to me and my big, pregnant belly. I wasn't exactly dressed for a night at the club. As a few of the employees started to recognize me, the word spread and I felt the crowd move back in slow motion to reveal him slumped against the bar, having a conversation, or trying to, with whoever was there.

My heart sank. My cheeks burned from the shame and embarrassment. I didn't know anything about emotional intelligence at the time, or about regulating my nervous system. I walked right up to him, trying to control my emotions, as well as my words. I pleaded with him to come home as he tried to convince me he was fine, slurring his words, his eyes struggling to focus on me.

I don't quite remember the walk home, but I do remember feeling the burden on my shoulders. I could feel the physical weight of the baby bump, of trying to hold him up and carry him back, all while slipping over the ice and tripping on the edge of the sidewalk. I could feel the emotional and physical weight of what had become my marriage, and my life.

At that point in my marriage, I honestly couldn't remember the good days anymore. Those days, the cycle devolved into the same old nightmarish groundhog day—I would ask him not to drink, he would promise he wouldn't, then he would break his promise. Again.

We'd fight about it, or rather I would bring it up, and he'd say, "Don't stress me out, I had a hard day at work," or some other excuse. I would stop talking to him for a couple of days. Eventually, I'd begrudgingly speak to him again because, well, life and three kids to raise together, and he would think he was forgiven but I would remain resentful.

Over and over again.

It's not like our life was awful. I know that from the outside it looked pretty perfect: two healthy kids, one more on the way, a stay-at-home mum, a great high-paying job for him. The expat life.

But on the inside, I couldn't stand it.

The constant worry about how drunk he'd get, if I would be there to do "damage control," if he would embarrass himself (and me) in front of his employees, if he'd end up in a ditch, or if he'd say something stupid to the wrong person and get beat up...

The constant empty broken promises, the underlying passive aggressive punishments I put on him through the silent treatment and the withholding of sex.

I just couldn't stand it anymore.

What happened? I struggled to understand why he couldn't see what it was doing to us. To our marriage. To our relationship. I thought I was doing a good job of hiding it from the kids, but who knows. I told him often, "Every time this happens you're chipping away at the iceberg, and one day there won't be any love left."

Why wouldn't he stop? Was I really asking for too much? Was it me who was being unreasonable? There's always a reason. An excuse.

"It's Monday, and it was a tough day at work."
"It's Tuesday and the big bosses are in. I'm so stressed."
"It's Wednesday, and the auditor was in."
"It's Thursday, so it's nearly the weekend, might as well 'celebrate.'"

I know I shouldn't complain. He didn't hurt me. He didn't cheat. He made good money, and by all means he seemed to love me very much. But I felt trapped. Unloved. To him, the alcohol was more important than me. Than our family. By now, we've been together for fifteen years and married for eight.

I just wanted a present husband. Someone I could count on to raise my kids with. Someone who would keep the simple promise he made regularly. The ironic thing is, I couldn't understand how that side of his personality coexisted with him being a (mostly) great dad. He was fun. He loved the boys and they adored him right back. He planned trips, and took them to discover new spots around the city. In his work life, he was a hard worker, ambitious, and very good at what he did—hotel management. He climbed the ladder over the years to get promotions and accolades.

Looking back now, I see the signs. The red flags were there when we met, I was just young and naïve. I thought if I loved him harder, if I changed who I was or if I tried to change him, if I could just *make him see* how much I loved him, he would understand and quit. Wouldn't he?

We nearly didn't make it a few times in our relationship. About five years in, I had a huge "there has to be more than this" moment.

I could start to see a pattern—we'd go out, he'd say he would only have a couple, and I would end up being the one who made sure we made it home, and got there safely. Somehow we always did, no thanks to him. I had a flash (or many, actually) of what my future would be, of doing this forever, pleading through our marriage, our parenthood, of this never ending cycle.

So, you ask.

What happened?

I've asked myself so many times.

Gosh, we were so young when we met. I was nineteen and he had just turned twenty. I remember the sparkle in his eye, the fun side of him, the laughter—he was cute and ambitious, which I loved. I knew I was going to live a life outside of the box—I wanted to grow in my work life, I wanted to travel. Live in different countries, raise my kids abroad, just like I had been as a kid. He also wanted to travel, he wanted to see the world, adventure, and had big plans for his career. We were a great fit.

A couple of months after we met, he left on a cruise ship—something he'd wanted to do forever—and I returned to Paris to finish my studies.

The love letters we wrote to each other in those few months were worthy of any Shakespearean literature!

Both our sets of parents thought they were rid of their child's young lover, but our story had only just begun. He would call me from the middle of the ocean, with a satellite phone that cost him $10 a minute. He shared his stories from the ship—the crazy storms, the wild things that guests do when they're stuck on a ship for days—and from the magical places he would visit along the way. The Bahamas, the Caribbean, South America, Mayan temples, you name it... he sure did travel the world.

He came home, and I finished my studies. He moved to Paris with me and learned French, to my mum's great satisfaction! Romantic, right? He lived in a "chambre de bonne" at the time; no room to swing a cat, five flights of stairs with no elevator, up which he carried his bike every day. Under the roofs of Paris' Place Des Vosges, where I had taken my first steps as a baby.

It should have worked.

I wanted it to work. I'm sure he wanted that, too.

Those early years in Paris then London... what a life. We traveled, we ate, we had so much fun. I suppose we got into a rhythm. Life was good(ish).

I remember in our first few months of dating, his grandfather passed away. We got on the train and went to stay with his sister to be with his family and attend the funeral. That was the first time I met his family. We didn't really think about it, I just went with him. On the day we arrived, his niece came home from pre-school and her whole face lit up when she saw him. The way he picked her up calling her "Princess," the way she squealed with delight. I thought right then and there that he was "father material."

But back to my question—what happened?

Where did we "go wrong"?

You know, I don't think we did.

At the time, I was in the thick of it all, and I spent a lot of energy making him wrong, making him the bad guy. I thought that made me the "good guy," but what I didn't realize was that making him the villain actually made me the victim. That by continuously repeating the same pattern, I was actually choosing to stay in it.

We didn't do anything wrong, we just grew in different directions.

I lost myself in motherhood for the better part of a decade, and didn't ever seriously think of leaving. The boys needed me, right? They needed me to be the parent who showed up because Dad was working. I'd said vows, to myself, to him, to God. I couldn't actually leave. Oh sure, I fantasized about it regularly. What would it feel like to not have this burden, this worry, how it would feel to live alone with the kids? But I couldn't let it get past that: a fantasy. Where would I go? How would I provide for myself and the boys? I'd been a stay at home mum for the better part of a decade. How would I handle a full time job and three kids that I would have to be the primary caregiver for? With his hotel hours, there was no way he would ever be able to pick them up from school, or help with their after school activities. How was I supposed to do that? That was the story I told myself for years. And so I forgave, over and over again. I'd give in and let go of my resentment, only to pick it up again a few days later, mad at him and mad at myself because nothing ever changed. Until one day, when I woke up after another overly boozy night, a night that should have been a fun celebration of the race we'd just completed together, but had ended poorly yet again.

I woke up and knew with every cell of my body that that was IT. This was the proverbial straw that broke the camel's back. It was the point of no return, when you know the iceberg has been completely chipped away at. There was nothing left. I knew I had nothing more to give. I knew I didn't have any more forgiveness left in me. I couldn't listen to another partial-apology, or go through another promise that would be broken. I knew I couldn't continue like this another ten years, never mind another six months.

"Pack your shit and go."

"What?"

I repeated myself, slower. "Pack. Your. Shit. And. Go."

I enunciated every word, making sure he could understand.

I was up at the side of the bed, trying to keep calm as I understood that this was the instant that my whole life, that our lives would change. The point of no return.

"What do you mean? Where will I go? What will we tell the boys?" His eyes were wide at the enormity of what I said. What I asked him to do sank in slowly, through the hangover I imagined he was nursing.

"I don't care where you go, figure it out. Pack a bag and get out. Now. I'll deal with the boys. I always do."

And so he packed a suitcase and drove off.

Instantly I felt calm. And in the very next second, I felt terrified. Anxious.

I could feel the certainty that this is how my story would unfold, that I've got this, that I was strong and I'll absolutely figure it out.

And I also felt a deep nagging fear, "What have I done?!" What *will* I tell the boys? My parents will be heartbroken."

Riding all these emotions one after another was like a crazy big roller coaster.

Somewhere in there I also hoped and prayed that this was just the kick up the butt he needed. An ultimatum to help him see I was serious, that there was a problem and it really did need fixing. The next step would be counseling or couples therapy. I had hoped we would get through it, and that he would get better so we could start again, stronger, together.

Sadly that wasn't how our story played out.

As I leaned against the door that closed behind him and shut my eyes, I heard the boys playing in their rooms. It was still early in the morning, and they were oblivious to what had just happened.

That first day went by as if he had just gone to work. There were regular weekends like that, where he would be working. It felt strangely "normal." The boys and I moved through our Sunday eating, playing, and watching a movie. That night after I'd put them to bed, I fell to my knees in the shower, sobbing. Reality set in. I was a single mum.

The next two years were a bit of a shit-show. He tried to come home numerous times, but refused to acknowledge the elephant in the room and wouldn't change or get help. I knew I had to hold onto my boundaries. I couldn't go back to living with him like that. My mental health depended on it.

I continued to focus on motherhood, holding space for the kids as they moved through this season of their lives, adjusting to their new reality. I spent no time looking after my own healing, nor did I make time for my own grief. Survival mode was activated. I had spent so much time focusing on what he was doing wrong that I hadn't looked at my part in it all. I didn't realize that I was allowed to pause, to take a breath and hold myself, to hold space for my pain and grieve the end of my marriage. I didn't realize I could grieve the life I thought I was going to have.

Now, don't get me wrong. When I say "my part in it," I do not for *one second* believe that I led him to drink, or that it was my fault. Although he did say that a few times, as a defense mechanism I guess. What I didn't realize at the time was that for me to attract and stay with someone like that, I had to have allowed it to a certain degree. I must have felt a certain way about myself. There must have been a certain level of codependency, and all that that brings with it. But I was so focused on surviving and on the kids that it took me some time to come to that conclusion, and do anything about it.

A lot of the early post-divorce years were spent biting my tongue and ignoring late night texts and phone calls. We figured out custody, work, and how to minimize (or at least, hold space for) the sadness the boys were feeling as they slowly discovered why I had left him.

Getting divorced is a full time job! There is so much to work out, especially with children involved. Even in a relatively amicable divorce, it might take a few emails back and forth to agree to the first thing. It's not just custody and how much time the kids spend with each parent, it's also how to split the holidays, who claims how many kids on their tax returns, who keeps or buys who out of the house, who gets the dog, the car.

So. Much. To. Deal. With.

On top of that, I had to field people's well meaning questions.

Where are you going to go?
I don't know, I'll figure it out.

What happened?
I'd rather not talk about it right now.

Did you try therapy?
Of course, we tried everything.

Aren't you worried you'll ruin the kids?
No, actually at this point I'm more worried that staying in this marriage would do that.

Wow, this is so sudden, have you thought this through?

To which I'd paste a cheesy smile on my face while every cell in my body screamed, and wanted to say, "SUDDEN??? Are you fucking KIDDING ME??? I've been going through this for YEARS!!!"

Here's a tip—if your friend is going through a divorce, *don't ask them these questions*. Your friend is probably trying to figure these things out, and feels like their head is about to explode. Don't ask what you can do to help—just show up. Be the one who's at the door with a bottle of their favorite wine, a big box of paper tissues, and the largest tub of ice cream you can find. Be the one whose shoulder they can cry on. Be there to help with the kids, or pack up the house, or make sure they are showered. Just be there. Don't ask a gazillion questions that they don't have the answers to. Don't be another thing that they have to deal with, or another person whose emotions they have to manage.

Ok. Rant over.

But back to the full-time job that is getting a divorce.

There's also going back to work. If you haven't been through this, let me tell you that re-entering the workforce as a woman who has been a full time mum of three in your forties and having spent most of the last decade raising your kids and elevating your husband's career, is not for the faint of heart. This in itself could warrant its own entire book. Phew.

Looking for work was an energy sucker I didn't have the bandwidth for. But I also needed to feed my kids. I was extremely overqualified for some of the jobs I applied for, which were minimum wage but close to home and would allow me to drop off and pick the kids up.

Or...

The jobs were middle-management hotel positions that required a 30-45 minute commute *each way*, and definitely didn't fit in with the boys' school day schedules. I couldn't even imagine going back to the hotel life I once knew. There's just not enough money in the world to be honest. If you know, you know.

So I took not one, but two of these minimum wage jobs. It wasn't the life I'd dreamed of, not even close. But then again, I'd never envisioned being divorced either.

The next few years after that were years of huge growth for me. I started to teach yoga, both public classes and with private clients. I built my business as well as my confidence. I "found myself" again as I did more and more things that lit me up. As I grew my yoga practice I also grew my healing practice by learning Reiki, and investing in myself with mentors and coaches. I trained as a Nutrition and Health Coach, then pivoted to Divorce Coaching as more and more women came to me looking for support when their marriages broke down. Somehow, I figured it out. Somehow, the boys and I made it through. We moved out of survival mode and found a rhythm again. We laughed again, and life went on.

So no regrets and no revenge, because without the life I had with him, without my divorce, I know I wouldn't have become the woman I am today. I may have never chosen to use my pain as a portal for transformation, and a reminder of who I really am.

Growth, expansion, and emotional maturity, how perfect, right? Well, unfortunately, I'm not about to give you the happy ending you may have been expecting.

Seven years after I asked him to pack his bag and leave, nearly to the day, I received a phone call on a Friday morning, just as I was about to take my youngest to school. It was a number I didn't recognize, but it was in my area code so I decided to answer.

"Hello?"

"Are you S's wife?"

There is no "hello," straight into the thick of it. I'm immediately on high alert.

"Umm kinda? Who is this?"

"This is Dr E from this hospital and S is here in the ICU. He came in last night, he's unconscious and we're trying to find out what happened. Can you give us any information?" The wheels in my brain start to turn at maximum speed while I try to process what this man just said.

A hospital.

The ICU.

Unconscious.

I don't understand.

What do you mean?

WHAT DO YOU MEAN???

I caught my son's eye, the question in his look. I had so many questions for this doctor and absolutely none of the answers he was looking for. I didn't know how he got there, I didn't know what he was doing before. No, I didn't know his daily whereabouts, or what kind of health insurance he had—we had been divorced seven years.

But yes, I did know that he broke that particular bone and had a plate in that area, and that he went through those two surgeries a while back. Yes, I authorized a blood transfusion and the request to start dialysis immediately.

The next five weeks were...well, I haven't yet found a word to describe that period. Crazy? Chaotic? Stressful? A blur? We went through all the emotions, and then some. I could only imagine what my kids went through. I made the conscious decision to divorce their father years ago. But for them, he still is and always would be their Dad.

In those five weeks, I moved through tasks like calling his family, after seven years of no contact. You can imagine how that conversation went. I helped them travel to us, and figured out their accommodations. In that same time, I also went from being asked to make huge medical decisions on his behalf, to being called by social services and told that as the ex-wife I had no rights to make them. Yikes. Cue connecting social services with his family who lived 7,500 miles away (yes, thousand, this isn't a typo) and with a twelve hour time difference.

The boys and I had to figure out how "normal" we wanted to keep our lives, and how much space we wanted to give ourselves (a lot!). What was the right thing to do? Newsflash, there is no right thing to do, only what's right for you, at any given moment.

We moved through life on a day by day basis, and on some days it was more of an hour by hour basis, deciding if we were going to "people" that day or if we wanted to "hermit." We were finding our balance between seeking support and seeking solitude.

It was the longest five weeks of our lives.

And then, the doctors told us he wouldn't make it.

Wait. No. No no no no no no no no.

NO.

WHAT?

How could that be? What did that mean? I didn't sign up for that, my kids didn't sign up for that! How would they live without their father?

I thought going through my divorce was the hardest thing I'd ever done.

I was wrong. Telling my children that their father had passed away absolutely topped that, and everything else I've ever lived through.

Our world as we'd known it ended that day. And it was never going to be the same again.

We weren't prepared. Five weeks wasn't enough time. No time would have been enough time. It's all a bit of a blur. Who am I kidding? It's a complete blur. And yet, clear as day, on the day he passed, I heard him.

"I'm ready."

"NO" I told him. "No, not now, not yet, we're not ready, how do I do this? How do I hold it all, how..."

Ironic how in his physical form he was the least "woowoo" person I've ever known, and the second he passed his voice came straight through.

"I'm ready now," he said again.

I gathered my things and went to pick the boys up early from school. You could have cut the silence in that six minute car ride home with a knife.

And then his voice came through to me again.

So clear, every time.

It was his voice, as if he were standing right in front of me.

"I am free now, and so are you."

As I fell to my knees and started to sob my heart out, I felt all at once the gratitude for his soul's freedom, and the grief for those of us he left behind.

The parents losing a child,
the children losing a father,
the sister losing a brother,
the friends losing a friend...

It wrapped me up with its velvety hand, and filled me up with the sadness that once was love.

I remember a few things quite vividly from those first few moments and days.

One thing that strikes me is how rude it feels that as one human is taking their last breath, life just goes on. As one family begins to grieve, others celebrate new life, new unions, and new exciting experiences. And in that instant it feels...well I can't think of another word. It feels rude. How *dare* you keep turning, Earth, as if nothing happened? Like my babies' father didn't just *die*??? What was I supposed to do with this bright sun, the bursts of laughter I heard from people on the street, the happy music playing on the radio? How could I grasp my children's sadness when I could barely hold my own?

Now, after some time has passed and things feel a little less raw, I honestly think, *thank God*. Thank God life does go on, and is there to catch us and get us back on the wagon of living. Thank God we get to continue to love, we get to laugh again, have another adventure. Thank God we don't stay stuck in a pit of utmost despair for the rest of forever. Our loved ones don't want us to cry until our last breath. They want us to live. They absolutely do.

Another thing I remember is the shock of how absolutely heartbroken I felt. Maybe it sounds weird to you reading this now, but I wasn't prepared for it. We're never prepared for someone to pass away, no matter their age. I never imagined he would leave us so suddenly and so soon, so it's not like I practiced how it would feel. But still, somehow I thought, with the work I'd done both on myself and the hundreds of clients I've worked with in moving through the grief that comes with a divorce, I guess...I don't know what I thought, actually. The heartbreak split me open. The sadness swallowed me up. The words from Marianne Williamson's book *A Return To Love* just kept replaying over and over again in my head.

"A return to love. Because once they're gone, what else is there?

Ashes to ashes, dust to dust. From love we came and to love we return."

What else am I to share with my kids but the love? I didn't want to rehash the past, spotlight the mistakes or relive our wounds. All I wanted for them was to remember all of his goodness. His ambition, that particular way his eyes sparkled when he laughed out loud, or how his nostrils would flare when he would tell a silly joke.

I will tell them the stories of their births and how he insisted on ironing his shirt, "for the photos" before he drove me to the hospital, how he pushed them too high on the swings until their tummies had butterflies. How he was always up for an adventure, the crazier the better, how he made the absolute best Gratin Dauphinois, and how I'd tease him by saying, "not bad for an English guy."

Because not only are the memories all we have left when they leave, but they are also how we keep them alive. Alive in our hearts, and alive in our memories.

That's another thing that hit me. When we pass away, that's IT. I mean I knew that, but then it happened and all that's left behind is just stuff.

As my closest girlfriends gathered to help me clean, pack up, and prepare his house for sale, I was hit by how all this stuff was just that—stuff. Clothes, toiletries, kitchenware, furniture, maybe some photos and pictures, trinkets from his travels. All. Just. Stuff. That's all we leave behind, along with the memories we created with others. Moments of life. Lived experiences. What we *truly* leave is how we made others feel. A word, a touch, a look, a shared joke. None of the material stuff matters.

So go live your life. Go create memories. Make sure your kids have lots to giggle about when you're gone. That way, when they talk about you, they can return to love. Feel you close.

I heard whispers early on after he'd passed. Whispers around me saying, "How tragic," or "Those poor boys," tossed in with words like "orphans" or "traumatized." I remember hearing it in a daze at the beginning, but as the veil started to lift slightly, I became very clear.

Absolutely not. No, thank you. Not on my watch.

I get it. People feel sorry, they think it is kindness, or they just think of how they would feel in this particular situation.

Don't.

I refuse the labels.

We are not just another statistic.

I am not a sad woman, I'm a happy woman going through sad times. It's the cycle of life.

The biggest lesson in all this?
LIVE.
Live your life loudly, joyfully.

Live because they couldn't.
It is not only your *birthright*, it is your *duty*.

Grief doesn't stop. Just because you felt a moment of joy or allowed yourself to laugh at a joke, or delight in the feeling of the sun on your skin, doesn't mean you've forgotten them. Grief is part of the life cycle. Death is part of the life cycle. Grief never ends, it just changes shape.

I remember one of my kids recently said, "I don't want to forget him." You never will, my love. You will never forget him. He is in every beat of your heart, in every twinkle of your eye, in every memory you hold of him and in every story you tell of him.

There is no one size fits all for grief. You're going to move through it at your own pace. Don't let anyone tell you that you're too happy too soon, or that you really shouldn't still feel so sad after whatever length of time.

It's your journey and you get to experience it however is most supportive for you.

I urge you to release any guilt. I want you to know that guilt is wasted energy. Don't feel bad because you haven't cried today, or because a laugh escaped you.

Your loved ones want you to live. They *urge* you to live.

As for us? We feel connected to him all the time. Every time his favorite songs play "randomly" on the radio or in the dentist's waiting room. Every time the curtains move, or the door flies open on a windless day, or every time our old cat, who lived with him for the last seven years, goes absolutely bonkers in the same corner right outside the boys room when there is nothing for the human eye to see...

I hear him all the time. He thanks me often, for raising our boys, for loving them, for keeping his memory alive with them.

He giggles at the fact that I tried so hard to get rid of all our furniture after our divorce and here I am, eight years later, with all of it in my house.

Connected.

It's what you choose to believe... you can see "just" a penny on the floor, or you can see a sign from your loved one. I know which one I prefer.

What do I choose to believe?
I believe in a return to love.

Although the last few years of our marriage weren't great, there were many good times, three beautiful boys came of it. While yes, our marriage came to completion, and we ended it, and our lives together felt messy and ugly at times, now that he's gone, none of that matters.

All that is left is love.

Audrey is a happily divorced mother of three who took the long route to healing, so that you don't have to. Her divorce in 2017 took her through some of her toughest times, some of which she didn't think she'd survive. She not only survived, but thrived through practices such as embodied yoga, mindset changes and reiki/energy work, and understood that her decision to leave her marriage hadn't broken her at all. It was transforming her into the version of herself she had been dreaming of for years: a bold, confident, powerful woman moving through life with clarity, grace and purpose. She became the Divorce Coach she needed in the early years of her own journey.

To connect with Audrey, visit iamaudreyalice.com, and follow her on instagram at @divorced.af.collective and @iamaudreyalice. You can also find her Podcast Divorced AF on apple podcasts and spotify.

3

CREATING OUR
"WE" SPACE

By Michelle Wincell O'Leary

When my newlywed husband threw his wedding ring across the living room, just missing my right eye, I could have ended things right then and there. He had become increasingly agitated at my insistence that he stand on his own and not depend on me as his primary source of validation. I metaphorically pulled him gently off of me, placed him on solid ground, and shared a perspective that changed our marriage. A choice that nearly destroyed my vision.

His glomming on to me felt like those clients who claimed to need me and only me to heal themselves. I've become an expert at remaining calm in the face of chaos. During my career as a mental health professional, I've neutralized many rooms and people with my energetic mastery of it. The resilience found in calm, quiet awareness offers an excellent observation point. Its protective stillness can stifle a volatile situation. Its stabilizing power allows consciousness itself to resurface.

Although he is thirteen years older, I'm the one who described how boundaries could hold our marriage together like pieces of a puzzle. I shared a vision where we each prioritized maintaining our sense of self and engaging independently with friends and personal interests. I emphasized how it would strengthen our marriage to feel grounded in our own identities.

I described how we'd grow into our marital bond through spending time together, enjoying co-creative dates, new adventures, and sharing about our experiences along the way. As I laid it out for him, I didn't expect him to gasp for air.

In the next moment, the hard-pitched platinum moved through the space between us in extremely slow motion. I felt like Trinity in *The Matrix*, watching as the bullet moved toward me and leaning ever so slightly to the left, my eyes followed its smooth passing to smack against the wall. As the metal crashed to the ground, the reverberations of cold, hard truth spread.

The disagreement itself disrupted and dissolved into dead stillness. Our timeline shifted so subtly in that void that I could have missed it if not for the deep ripples. The living room events felt out of sequence. My seated posture lengthened in my stunned calmness, while across the room, he loomed in front of the wide-screen television.

No fucking way.

How can I possibly be in this place again?

What just happened?

What in the hell am I going to do now?

Tell him in absolute terms that this will never happen again.

I heard my inner commanding voice and used it to deliver the warning. "This is the only time you will ever behave this way."

I watched as my words sank into his awareness.

Moments ago, he'd been performing to seduce me into his desires, dancing around as he spun tall tales. "Come with me. It will be fun. Everyone will be there." His act played like a jolly leprechaun, all smiles and rainbows. He actively attempted to hide his desperation for my appearance, his opportunity to sparkle up his ego. He wanted the admiration of his audience. It had nothing to do with me.

I saw clearly through it, knowing the game being played. His concept of companionship felt collared and leashed. He even pouted with his puppy dog eyes.

You're a big boy.

I'm not falling for this.

Seriously?

He was all charm and wit as he painted a pleasurable canvas certain to entice me and then, a fireworks-style call to action. I must go! I was his wife! I must prove my love and demonstrate it for all to see! I must dote on him and puff him up! The expectations circled like echoes through my mind.

Validate him.

Help him to be admired by others.

Satisfy his desire to feel worthy.

Complete him.

His ingrained beliefs were self-evident: Married people accompany each other to gatherings regardless of the activity, event, timing, location, or who else is attending. None of my sub-context mattered. Except that it did matter—to me.

I think you've forgotten who you married.

Complete yourself.

I'm certainly not a wallflower or side piece you can parade around whenever it suits you.

Not someone you can guilt into action.

I have a choice.

I choose no.

It triggered something in him. He removed and blasted his ring at me without a pause to consider the potential damage. It was obvious that my 'no' elicited an automatic reaction. It was so out of proportion that it was bewildering, though not for long. At least, not to me.

It's not only what I witnessed him do, but how I sensed he felt about himself doing it. An image of his regression flashed through my mind. He was a young boy being rejected by his mother and seeking to destroy her for it. I instantly knew his behavior was not about me. He was in the past, unconscious, reenacting a story that always ended the same.

His sadness was a cold river flowing deep within.

I was a tree, with roots extended to the center of the Earth.

I did not flinch. I uttered not one sound, at first. I simply directed my shocked lips to come together, narrowed my wide eyes, and calmly waited as he began to recognize what he'd just done. One hand went to his hip while the other opened up across his forehead, soothing himself as he considered becoming invisible within his shame.

The power of my warning illuminated the gravity of the moment. We looked at each other as time stretched out, settling us into our consciousness. I don't remember exactly what happened next, only that I had reclaimed my sovereignty. I felt certain he had received the fullness of my notice because he looked stunned, carefully stepping back and out of the battlefield. I remember that.

What I wanted was to have a meaningful conversation with him about our differences, balance, freedom, and other marital ideals. I was aware that his highly social nature and my quiet intensity coexisted incongruently. Through an open discussion, he could nudge me out of my comfort zone, while I assuaged his persistent longing for approval. I yearned for us to unearth our marital rhythm.

But those desires were paused. The dream shifted. In my shock, I had jumped out to drive a stake into sacred ground. My *'never again'* message was as serious as the presence of the grim reaper. There wasn't one hair on his furry body that did not stand up to notice. My warrior spirit had temporarily taken over.

You will not take my power away.

You are not in charge of me.

You will not destroy me.

I will not lose my sense of self.

You will want to discover your own.

The truth is, I was wildly in love with him. I'd known him for more than a decade before we dated. When I first laid eyes on him, he charmed me with smiling eyes and a dark suit jacket. Dressed in my long, brick-red leather skirt and tall black boots, I greeted him with a warm smile. He had arrived for a job interview, and as we sat together in my small therapy office, I realized that I couldn't hire him. He was too recent a graduate for the role. Nevertheless, we talked and laughed our way through an "interview" that we would not forget.

Some ten years later, when our paths crossed at one of my workshops, he asked me to a 'lunch meeting.' As a fellow therapist, he was curious about my therapeutic entrepreneurial endeavors. We sat facing each other at a small square table covered by a red and white checked cloth. Our conversation was easy and comfortable. We laughed our way through Jasmine tea and spicy Thai dishes. He asked all kinds of questions that I answered thoughtfully.

I inquired about his experience as one of the few male therapists in our field. As he talked, I zoomed in to examine what I thought was a wedding ring, and discovered it was actually a sterling ode to Harley-Davidson on his finger. I was intrigued. Our 'meeting' shifted gears when he inquired what I liked to do outside of work. I happily shared stories of my travels, friends, and interests. I played along.

Shortly thereafter, I was surprised when he admitted to signing up for my workshops over the years to "keep tabs on me." I recalled seeing him in the audience, smiling at me. Our attraction struck like ashes in a fire.

Wait, I thought this was a business meeting?

What is happening?

Damn, he's handsome. And that smile!

Focus. Be cool.

I blushed when he suddenly inquired if I was married. He noticed that I was also not wearing a wedding ring, and that I hadn't mentioned a partner in my stories. In synchronized harmony, we exclaimed, "I thought you were married!" The heat between us ignited as thoughts about his motives popped into my mind.

So you asked a possibly married woman on a date disguised as a business lunch?

Or perhaps you noticed the missing wedding ring before you asked?

Hmmmm...?

He was quick-witted as he relayed that having lunch with me, even if I were married, would still be a worthwhile use of his time. He was smooth.

I'm the one who's not smooth.

I hoped he would miss how flushed and tongue-tied I'd become. To settle my anxious excitement, I quickly excused myself to return to work. As we parted ways along the city street, his gaze never left me as I walked coolly back to my car. I drove off in a happy fog.

Our first meeting was filled with excitement and the possibility of something new. It almost doesn't make sense how we jumped from that first lunch to tense newlyweds. We were navigating our rhythm when misalignments exploded in our space. Then, we simply closed it up as if it never happened.

But the ripples of the ring incident stretched out far. He stopped asking me every time he went out to come along. I would choose not to go, and he would reluctantly accept. My independence was creating a wedge between us.

I played the free introductory video of A Course In Mastering Alchemy for him as a potential consciousness-building program for *us*. This time, I was the one excited to present an activity that I felt certain would be an amazing experience for us. He followed my lead, smiling as he curiously watched and listened.

What was there to lose?

There's nowhere to go but forward, right?

What could go wrong?

I didn't stop to consider my question. He agreed to take the course with me, so I jumped to registration and paid the fee. I wanted to get started right away on our shared alchemy quest.

This could be the beginning of something good.

In my awareness, I'd shifted to doubt.

I feel like I've heard this somewhere before.

I'd arrive at the living room first, anticipating his arrival and sensing his mood as he strolled in. He'd plop on the far side of our faux leather couch, leaving each of us nestled in like opposing magnetic forces. Jim Self, our Mastering Alchemy guide, appeared overly large for his small stature on the television screen connected via laptop. His voice, eyes, and energetic presence simply tuned in to me like I was the one connected by a cable. I was immediately, completely drawn in.

The opening activity was for each of us to create and hold a clear intention of becoming fully conscious and knowing ourselves. I was immersed in setting my intention and then, for a quick moment, I peeked and found his eyes closed as he quietly concentrated. He assumed a cross-legged position on the couch, his palms facing up and gently resting on his knees as if to receive. That brought a smile to my already softened heart, hopeful for our future.

After setting our intentions, I shared my experience. It felt like a new beginning, an awakening that for me enlivened with fascination. It was curiously soothing to hold conscious awareness of myself. I found Jim completely mesmerizing with his nuanced, energetic mastery. I didn't know exactly what I was doing, but I followed the energetics intuitively, sensing new awareness in every moment.

He was less enthusiastic than I was. His usual animated flair had morphed into a contemplative quietness. I assumed it was a side effect of our meditative intention-setting. He was pleasantly agreeable as he uneventfully left the room, leaving me alone on the couch in my reflective, peaceful bliss.

I am so ready for this.

Wait, I think I just noticed being aware of being aware of myself.

I could do this every day.

When I arrived back on the couch that following week, I sat elegantly in my corner like a queen on her throne. I imagined him walking in adorned by a crown over his balding hairline, although his entrance resembled more of a court jester, juggling teacups, notebooks, and a laptop. I was thrilled he had returned for our second royal class. I was ready to experience more.

Jim directed us to notice ourselves being quiet. With another breath, we sensed the feeling of being present, and then slowly moved into our awareness. Our still energies merged with the sunlight that streamed in through the large picture window. The diffused light drew us into our conscious awareness. It felt light and airy.

Jim pointed us to practice how to look from behind our eyes, from the center of our heads. We shifted our focus to noticing the difference between seeing and looking. We'd see the broad, wide view in front of us and then zoom in to look at the details. As we played, the clarity of new perspectives held our attention. It was incredibly powerful.

When we finally noticed each other from across our thrones, it felt different. We were more present, and our grounding was firmer and more stable. I realized that I was seeing beyond his royal corner because *his* energies were no longer my focus. I looked into myself to notice my nuances. I'd shifted my perspective.

I wonder if he's having this kind of experience?

Is he looking beyond me, too?

"That was fun!" he offered up cheerfully, shrugging his shoulders. His sudden words jostled me out of my meditative fascination. He must have had somewhere else to be. His quick departure left questions unasked and unanswered, like a mid-sentence dropping off. I sat, pondering without thought. I looked out the picture window and noticed more than I had noticed before.

Both of us being therapists were uniquely privileged to have sacred views into the inner workings of others. When we came together as a couple, our protective shields slowly went up as if to conceal our vulnerabilities. It was like thick clouds circled us, and we held them close to safeguard against the knowing eye of the other. Inside, we kept our most cherished secrets. To escape being found out, he'd dart out of a room or conversation, much like when I rushed out of our first date. We employed mutual defense mechanisms to maintain our sense of safety.

I felt safe arriving early to the couch. I'd set my energies and the tone of the room. I watched how my intentions impacted my experience. On one occasion, I noticed his more subdued entrance. The holes in his t-shirt signaled it was a favorite, a comfort to him. He carried two cups of hot tea and offered one to me. After taking a small sip, he plopped his feet up and leaned back. I pondered the purpose of the comforts he brought with him.

The aroma of fresh jasmine filled the room, widening my smile. It triggered joy for my expanding conscious awareness and sweet memories of our first unofficial date. If he intended to bring comfortability to our learning experience, it worked.

My connection with Mastering Alchemy was somehow familiar, like the feeling of returning home. Jim's energetic presence pointed to a new spiritual path, one that would lead to some magical place. I hoped this magic sparked for my husband, too. I wanted a shared mystical journey with him.

I'm sending you vibrations of comfort.

I'm sharing sparks of joy and wonder.

I'm grateful that you're here.

Jim led us in grounding and becoming quiet and aware in our presence, as we moved back to examine the center of our heads. Jim asked if we'd ever experienced someone jumping into the center of our heads. He told us how common this was. Like when someone shames you, or tells you in some way that you're not okay and you believe it as if it were true. You unconsciously agree to become not okay, as they take over the center of your head.

The exercise went something like this: Ask yourself, "Who is in the center of my head?" Without questioning, hear the first name that pops into your awareness. No judgment.

Not right or wrong. Whoever the name is, just intend to clear it out of your head. Tell them to leave. Repeat this as many times as a name pops up when you ask, "Who is in the center of my head?"

Then own the center of your head. It's your command center. Your reality where you are in charge. Make yourself a beautiful space there, a little environment that's entirely comfortable and recognizable for you. Own it.

What the hell?

My parents, my boss, my son, my friends, and of course, my husband were all in the center of my head. Repeatedly.

Do this, don't do that, think this, don't think that, hurry up, change this, change that – utter nonsense!

One by one, over and over, everybody out!

Wait, I wonder if I'm in the center of his head?

I'm sure that I am.

It's not a problem, though, I heard Jim say. No judgment. It's just awareness.

It's ok. I'm ok.

Breathe.

Own it.

We turned inward from our polar opposite armrests, sheepish after practicing silently alongside one another. We agreed that the experience was oddly quick in discovering who was in there seeking control. We could feel sensations shifting in our awareness and bodies as we cleared out our head centers. I was happy with our openness. It was like owning the center of our heads brought our voices back, and we used them. It was a good start.

Ahhhh, I like this "us."

I can't believe all the noise of other people in the center of my head.

We left the rest unsaid. Who were all those in our heads? I think we knew. We preferred avoiding uncomfortable truths that might spark potential disagreements. We liked our cloud veil. Sometimes, good was good enough. It progressed in small steps. We would sail smoothly on good enough, for a while.

Just focus on my intention to know myself, and breathe.

Be in the center of my head and look out through my eyes, and just notice.

There's my smile.

Exhale.

And don't forget to inhale.

Own it.

Over the next several weeks, I'd look into his energy when he engaged in alchemy play. One day, I noticed that he chose to sit in the antique armchair across the room. With the couch to myself, I was at the farthest possible distance from him. Between us was more space for our energies to expand. We started class as usual, being quiet, present, and aware. We engaged in a grounding exercise that, for me, felt ineffective due to my noisy internal chatter.

I wonder if he noticed my disappointment?

He chose that chair for a reason, knowing the distance between us would be obvious. Right?

Why is he more comfortable sitting over there?

It's ok. I like my space. I like me. I'm comfortable being myself.

Keep telling yourself this.

At least he's here.

Good enough.

I sent useless telepathic messages, pleading, "Jim, please bring us some wisdom!"

Wait—who's in the center of my head?

Ah, there he is. Out you go.

Own it. It's yours.

We were immediately transported into a pivotal teaching of one of the most important tools in Mastering Alchemy, 'the Rose.' We each envisioned a long-stemmed red Rose and placed it at the edge of our auras to help us define where we each hold our energetic space. We stood across from each other, practicing moving around within our Rose-defined personal spaces.

Then, to learn how flexible our roses and spaces were, we moved in closer to one another and gauged our comfort levels. As we moved even closer still, our Rose defined spaces condensed, and we remained comfortable. Aware within our spaces, we glanced knowingly at each other. We played like a couple of dancing bubbles. It was fun. Until it wasn't.

We inched closer until we felt it was near enough. We stopped at our closest mutual point of comfort, a Rose centered in the space between us. For some couples, a Rose might be as close as the tip of their nose, but that wasn't our comfort zone. Still, we were oddly close, given our very spacious seating arrangement today.

Jim smoothly transitioned to a description of the "we" space. Our "we" space is an energetic bubble between us that we can both step into and fill with agreements we choose as a couple. It holds our shared beliefs and desires, and anything else we both agree to fill it with. This concept resonated with me. I was intrigued.

Energetically, Jim demonstrated how to walk around in our own energy space and then consciously enter the sacred "we" space. He presented a respectful, co-creative process of discovering and creating our "we" space exactly as *we* desired. I focused on holding gratitude for our "we" space as I consciously stepped back into my personal energy field. My excitement blossomed, and then shifted with new awareness.

This is incredible!

It's exactly what I've always wanted; it's even better!

Oh, no!

The ring incident! This is what I was talking about!

This may not go over well.

Now he's hearing about boundaries from someone else!

He's hearing about this from Jim, in the class that I suggested we take.

Breathe...Ground...Center...

It seemed obvious that the "we" space mirrored my heartfelt desires for our marriage, although I silenced my voice. I held the quiet, calm space for him to recognize this sacred potential for himself. Perhaps he'd appreciate the concept more because it didn't come from me. Maybe it was the universe offering us a golden opportunity.

Are you noticing?

Are you with me?

Hello?

Crickets...

Finally, out of the silence, my husband surprised me when he suggested we take a seat on the couch. He moved in at a distance that mirrored our comfort zone of moments earlier. We held a Rose between us. He leaned back, took a deep breath, and began.

What he shared in that closeness was not what I wanted to hear. I knew that he'd likely prepared the message before our "we" space session. I also knew that the experience of it had moved its priority into the present moment. I held back tears, sad that he was unable to recognize the opportunity in front of him.

He shared the logic of his decision. To him, the alchemy classes seemed similar to his prior learnings of transcendental therapies and alternative philosophies.

Nothing struck him as remarkable, new, or different. He wasn't all that keen on Jim's teaching style either, finding him goofy and awkward. "I gave it a shot," he remarked, "and it didn't connect for me."

So, there it was. He's out.

He already knows everything about everything.

Blame it on Jim's style.

I shook my head in disappointment, unable to find words. He supported my continued involvement. He could see that it was important to me. He noticed how my eyes lit up when Jim was teaching.

It just didn't connect for him. He believed it was as simple as that. In some ways it was, and he overlooked the potential to strengthen our connection. Logic doesn't understand that.

If it doesn't connect for you, then it doesn't connect us.

Hmmm, are you by chance competing with Jim for my attention?

Are you rejecting this opportunity because it's so aligned with me?

Oh, there it was. His need for validation again and my stake energetically and unconsciously are still between us.

I'm the bad mom, remember?

Unless I give him my full attention, he's not worthy—and neither am I.

And neither is whatever or whoever I am giving my attention to.

The unconscious agreements in our "we" space screamed for their release. Lingering there were all the 'not good enoughs' we each felt in our disappointment with each other and ourselves. It was too much for us to consciously awaken to in the moment. We'd take another step back and not talk much about Mastering Alchemy for a while. Our quiet choices created more distance between us than we allowed into our awareness.

I continued the alchemy classes and regularly practiced using energy tools. I began waking early for meditation during the illuminated sunrises. I joined evening and weekend collectives of higher conscious awareness as we engaged with spiritual evolution. I played with sacred geometries and the energies of colors, sounds, and words. I became conscious of being unconscious and capable of intentionally shifting into being conscious.

I began to carefully examine my patterns, thoughts, emotions, actions, and experiences. I tuned in to discover misalignments of who I had become with who I truly wished to be. It was a conscious decoding game to discern what I was holding onto that no longer fit and had no value in the present. In my growing consciousness, I began to intentionally change.

Consciously remembering who I am has been the most meaningful experience of my life. It's extraordinarily powerful to consciously release who I no longer wish to be, and even more so to become the creator of my life, on my terms. The original intention to know myself manifested.

I release all my versions of being a victim. There is nothing useful in those energies for me.

I let go of abandonment, not being loved, not being worthy, not being good enough, and all the related beliefs and experiences for which there is no value to me now.

Instead—I like me, I am capable, I am worthy, I deserve, and I give myself permission to experience what I desire. These hold value for me. I am conscious that I am conscious.

As I walked through the small hallway that connected two bedrooms, I was surprised by the scene.

What is he doing there?

How long has he been sitting?

Is he meditating?

He'd begun mirroring my practices, sitting in meditation in his corner of our small cottage. All of his miniature tchotchkes, those ancient tokens of wisdom he'd collected through the years, surrounded him. Soft lighting gently illuminated his cross-legged position and closed eyes. I hadn't ever seen him sit still for that long. He looked peaceful.

Hmmm? This is new!

I wonder if my energies are having an impact on him?

Maybe he's noticed changes in me, and wants to change too?

Perhaps he wants me to notice and validate him.

He left the door open.

I validated his efforts to connect with himself. We enjoyed spontaneous conversations about our meditations. We each intentionally pursued our spiritual path and transitioned to a new way of being with ourselves and each other. A new rhythm had emerged.

In the bubbling up of our new energies, we could have easily missed the unexpected, profound moment when we found ourselves back on our couch. We'd chosen to watch a B-movie, *The Lobster* with Colin Farrell as the lead. The film was set in another reality where individuals were matched with their lifelong partners when a mutual passion was discovered. You could be paired with a total stranger when it's learned that you both have a passion for trains, for example. Just like that, and you're considered to be mates for life, like lobsters.

Somehow, we saw a new future for ourselves through that film. It begged us to answer the question, "What's our Lobster?" The movie was so strange that we didn't believe it could have significance for us. We posed possibilities for fun. "What about vacationing? Or camping? Maybe motorcycles? We enjoyed theme parties? We're both Irish?" Our "we" space suddenly illuminated with our commonalities.

To be sure, we had all those things in common, but they fell flat as shared passions. We paused to allow our epiphany to surface, and suddenly there it was. We both loved boating! "Yes," we shouted! Our Lobster was our love of being on the water!

No way!

Our Lobster!

Memories of our many boats brought smiles to our faces. Sailboats, power boats, even a jet boat cruised through our minds. We'd given up boats with motors years ago, at my request, when boat after boat had engine problems. We'd wait in line to launch for hours only to hear the dead silence of our motor.

Our passion for boats, motors, and getting back out on the water was easily rekindled. We were bursting at the seams with excitement.

I also hoped our passion for each other would be rekindled through our Lobster.

"Let's start looking at boats! What kind of boat should we get?" we pondered. He'd always loved sailing, and sailboats are less reliant on motors. "Let's go for it!" We agreed. Finding our Lobster as we were also finding our spiritual selves, felt destined.

The next week, I sold my beautiful golden Triumph motorcycle to purchase our sailboat! We'd found a twenty-six foot MacGregor in bright blue and white. We secured the last slip available at our first choice of marinas along the Mississippi River. I was so excited that I began high-intensity workouts so I could jump around the boat and handle the dock lines. I wanted to feel comfortable in a bikini under the hot marina sun. It was a shocking, sudden shift for us.

Out of nowhere, we're boating again?!

It's meant to be!

There's a bulge in the Mississippi River that's simultaneously a large, gorgeous lake. It's well known by sailors and everyone who's ever been there. It's a strikingly beautiful stretch of river anchored by several low-profile river towns.

It holds unusual sacred energies of the ice age in an area that never actually froze over. The "Driftless Area" was never flattened by glaciers, leaving the river deep and beautiful bluffs in their natural state.

It became our new home away from home. Our tiny floating cabin. Our slice of heaven. A divine setting for our unconscious marriage to transform.

I took my role as first mate seriously and learned the basics of sailing. I bought him a captain's hat that he wore with pride. Our Lobster had become our reality.

This is too good to be true.

Don't put that negative energy out there.

Good point.

In reality, our little boat had barely enough room for us. To acquire any one item from its specific location took several steps. Once we mounted the kitchen table in place, for example, we'd no longer have access to the kitchen cabinets. It was a small, specifically functional space, and we loved it, for a while.

We somehow believed that just being on the water would be enough to flow our relationship toward a deeper connection. Yet the emotional distance between us seemed as wide as the vastness of the twenty-two mile lake. Our conversations inevitably revisited our usual pain points, those unconscious placeholders popping back into our awareness despite our floating bliss.

"Maybe we should see a couples therapist," my husband, who was a couples therapist, said to me as we sailed into the wind. It wasn't the first time.

"What do you think they will suggest that we do?" I asked knowingly. It was the same response I'd given every time he'd suggested this.

They will suggest that we talk with each other and identify what's going on between us.

We'd be advised to become vulnerable and talk about our feelings.

Here we were with *the* perfect opportunity to talk with each other, and instead we jumped right back into old arguments, sitting right where we'd left them. Then, we'd stop talking altogether and simply observe the beauty of nature. We longed for our tension to quietly float away and leave us to our relaxation. We just wanted to be happy.

Sailing is not necessarily relaxing. It requires attention, focus, and quick decisions that depend primarily on shifting winds. Opportunities for arguments were blowing in the wind, testing our patience despite our decades-long careers as therapists. As sailors, therapy skills had little value.

Our windy adventures reminded me of an idea. I called it 'Water Therapy' and it was simple. We'd head out on the lake and just talk, opening up while immersed in the quiet freedom of nature. It was private and spacious on the water. We could allow ourselves to be vulnerable and unrushed.

So we floated. "What do you want to talk about?" we asked the other. We'd consider subjects that felt safe. We'd become a little braver and more open with every conversation.

It feels good to enjoy each other's company.

I'm happy we are still friends.

I wonder why it's taking us so long to explore deeper topics?

To make a real difference, we needed to go deeper.

"Ok, I'll go." I wanted to move us to the actual issues. "We haven't been intimate for a while now."

Like for years...

I wasn't sure what to say after dropping the elephant in our "we" space. It wasn't as eloquent a delivery as I'd imagined it to be.

At least I didn't finish the sentence out loud.

He jumped in defensively, "That's your fault. You're the one who told me to stop," he blasted.

How can I tell him that I've been traumatized without him taking it personally?

Can this not become an argument, please?

My past issues resurfaced as I was unraveling myself— would he understand that?

Somehow, my words would not form audible sentences, so I shifted my approach. "We tried again when we were in Florida, remember?"

"We had a fun time at a nice hotel along the ocean. A great day at the beach..." I stopped mid-sentence.

Oops, bad choice. Florida didn't end well.

"I remember you pulling away," he reminded me as if I needed reminding.

"We talked about that. Something didn't feel right with me." I felt hopeless in my faltering attempts to share what was on my mind. That night in Florida, our passion lasted for one quick minute. He felt distant, like a stranger. I stumbled into telling him that he was more like a friend to me than a lover. We'd grown apart after years of intimate distance.

I can't just turn it back on like a light switch, I'd told him.

I needed to reconnect emotionally, even spiritually, first. I told him this, too.

I attempted to express my thoughts, but mutual frustration ended our conversation. We tuned in to the beautiful lake and just floated in our own bubbles. We soaked up the sun and dozed off under puffy shade clouds. Later, we'd lie side by side in our tight sleeping quarters and feel a million miles apart.

At least we were on the water.

At least the elephant finally appeared. That was a truth that we'd need to unweave and reweave to rekindle our passion. For now, we each drifted into dreams, rocking softly on the water.

Our tenuous water therapy was soothed by the beauty that surrounded us. We found peace in the quiet. I shared how emotional connection could help us to resume being physically intimate. I hoped we'd have sex again and christen our floating tiny cabin, but that never happened.

Our continued misalignments showed up in arguments about the boat, the weather, or anything other than the emerging consciousness of our emotionally disconnected relationship.

I had another idea. It seemed like a good Hail Mary. "What about a bigger boat?" I threw it out there.

The idea served as a new beginning for our unconscious marriage to transform. I'm quick with ideas aligned with excitement, and he loves shiny new toys that come with two 350-motors. So we set off exploring and quickly found a bigger boat we both loved. We were instantly mesmerized and knew it was the one!

If we don't have sex on this boat, we never will.

Imagine water therapy on this lush party deck!

I can't believe this is our beautiful new Lobster!

It was the perfect size at thirty-two feet, and a four foot swim deck. It wasn't a sailboat, but it gave us room to breathe. The luxurious party deck was an ideal hosting space, and below deck had all the comforts of a bigger floating home. It even had a spacious sleeping area with a window that opened to the stars. It was elegant and smooth.

We upgraded to luxury water therapy. We had motored to a preferred spot and anchored. I'd prepare lunch, and we'd enjoy an ice-cold beverage. We'd sit back and kick up our feet while the boat floated buoyantly. We basked in the sun and the feeling of our Lobster, while our distant intimacy floated alongside.

"Anything you want to talk about?" one of us might inquire.

"Another beautiful day in paradise," the other might happily respond.

Aaaahhh. Yes. Nothing more to say.

I relished my morning alchemy meditations at sunrise, overlooking the lake. I delved deeper into my conscious awareness while he slept below deck. He'd surface and I'd point to my earbuds to let him know I was listening to a session. He'd grab his coffee and sit quietly for a few moments, eventually leaving for morning conversations with other sailors. We each found a new rhythm, and the season wrapped, void of intimacy.

Maybe next year...

That winter, everything changed. Coronavirus affected nearly everyone on the planet, and we were no exception. I purchased a desk and chair for a nook in the corner of the living room, unaware that I'd begin using it the very next day. My career was spent working in an office, and then boom, I was working from home. I'd never return to my former ways of working or being.

During COVID, there'd be periods when we both worked from home, stuffed into our small 1950s cottage together for days, weeks, and then months. The small space we shared barely contained us. We'd become comfortable having room to ourselves. Suddenly, being together all the time left us both feeling uneasy.

I was grateful that energy meditations soothed and comforted me. In the energetic space of quiet, present, and awareness, I would become conscious of myself. I tuned everything else out. I could just be.

I often found solace in the hot tub we'd situated in our half-acre backyard. I soaked for hours while listening to alchemy meditations. Sometimes he joined me, and before we knew it, we were in a different version of water therapy. I'd share about my latest alchemy fascination while he listened. He looked older, tired, and stressed while submerged in the tub. We'd end up in various conversations as the steam surrounded our floating bodies.

We'd eventually drift off into our thoughts. In the quiet, I imagined a new life for myself. I waited until conversations about the next boating season naturally came up. Then, I casually tossed it out there, "Hey, I have an idea. Since I'm 100 percent remote, I'd like to work from the boat this year!"

Who wouldn't want to work from a boat?

"What better place could there be to be quarantined from COVID exposure?" I added, though I didn't need to because he had already nodded in agreement.

He wouldn't be able to join me because he was providing in-person client sessions. I assumed that would be the case. I imagined we'd both be happy to have some alone time back.

Are you sure?

He said he didn't mind.

I am so excited!!

We agreed to shift back into our comfort zone. It relieved our tension so we could breathe again. That's the vision we had. We didn't worry about where it could lead.

As the boat splashed in, I could barely contain myself. I had space for quiet meditations, runs and yoga alongside the river, and I could just peacefully float. We'd spend weekends together, and Sunday afternoon would come quickly. He'd give me a peck goodbye and walk with a pep down the dock for his beloved motorcycle ride home. Win-win.

He'd eventually inquire about when I would be coming home. I'd talk around it, my words garbled. It didn't matter, I told myself. We enjoyed having space for ourselves. This arrangement would serve us well. We could miss each other, and have more to talk about when we reconnect.

I'm just going to stay at the boat.

I'm not coming home.

I have everything I need right here.

I'm happy.

My alchemy sessions were extremely expansive, floating in the vast natural beauty I was immersed in. Territorial calls of eagles became nature's signal that the sun would soon be rising. I'd prepare a freshly ground French press and meditate in the gorgeous sunrise colors. Working remotely felt like a breeze, uninterrupted and comfortable. After a light lunch, I'd take a quick catnap lying on the port deck like a teenager in my bikini. Living on a boat felt like a dream.

This is living.

Why don't I do this all the time?

I began to realize that I could create more and more freedom from expectations of the world around me. Sometimes in the quiet, I recalled unasked and unanswered questions from long ago.

What was there to lose?
My past.

There's nowhere but forward, right?

True, and not exactly. Stillness is a form of forward, centered, right in the present moment. I didn't have to move anywhere. I could elevate into higher dimensions from my still, conscious center while floating on the river.

What could go wrong?

It's not about right or wrong. It's about my truth. What feels right to me. What do I want to create for myself in this present-moment life I'm living? Who do I want to be?

Without fully intending to, I'd shifted into a new life. A different timeline moved into my flow. Blame it on COVID; it was the perfect opportunity to reimagine how to live. I gained back hours a day by working remotely, and now I was living on a boat!

I had fully embraced my expanding consciousness, recognized my interconnectedness with nature, and found the wisdom of my higher self. I had always been here, in my center, where I was meant to be. I just needed to remember how to find myself. Once I did, there was no turning back.

To amplify my husband's enjoyment of *his* present moments, I focused on preparing everything for his arrival. I washed the boat, planned the meals, purchased groceries, bought liquid refreshments, and had everything prepared and waiting for him. All he had to do was enjoy a motorcycle ride to join me, and be greeted with a drink, a hug, and a smile aboard our floating luxury getaway. It felt like the perfect Lobster experience.

So I was surprised when our same-old unconscious conversations and ineffective solutions resurfaced once more.

"Why aren't you coming home?" was what I expected to hear.

"We should get a bigger boat," is what I heard.

"Excuse me? I'm taking care of everything here, all you have to do is show up and enjoy yourself!"

I thought I'd heard it all—his hip hurt, his arm fell asleep during the night, the boat seating wasn't comfortable—the litany of complaints was a never-ending parade. I was astounded. I was also fully conscious that we were arguing about the boat's discomfort instead of addressing our disconnected and uncomfortable lives.

Here we go again.

There is no way we are getting a bigger boat.

I wanted freedom from repeated arguments and dated norms that no longer held value. The financial strain of a bigger boat had no value. Even the contractual part of our marriage seemed unnecessary. I didn't need an office or even employment, which drained my energy with broken systems. I envisioned a new life built on well-being and freedom!

Instead of a bigger boat, I spun the conversation on its head. "How about a legal dissolution of our marriage? We don't need a contract to be together." I never actually believed it would end our relationship. I assumed we'd continue as is, occasional boat complaints and all. I didn't value having a meaningless contract as the basis of our marriage.

Marriage, as with all of my endeavors, is personal, not contractual. Our marriage stopped being intimate more than five years ago. Our friendship remained intact, and our "we" space was fun. Our lobster was a beautiful experience, even though it didn't revive the passion we used to feel for each other.

What's the difference? No contract, no unnecessary complications.

We don't have to change anything other than the legal contract that no longer serves us. It's very simple.

Or...hmmm...is now the right time to ask?

What the hell.

What do I have to lose?

And there it was.

"You know, we could consider having an 'open' marriage. We can create whatever we want."

There. I did it. I said it.

We could open up our "we" space, clear it out, and step into a new conscious marriage defined by us. Start over. Recreate it. Make our own rules.

My life has transformed. I'm not the me I used to be. I'm more me than ever!

Shit hit the proverbial fan. I'd said it, 'open marriage.' There it was in plain sight. It must have felt to him like I picked up that wedding ring he flung all those years ago and pummeled it right back in his face, because he lost his freaking mind.

"I will leave you before I will ever have an open marriage," he firmly declared in anger.

"Why? You're a hippie from the sixties, isn't that a part of your coming of age culture?" I tossed that in as if there was room for persuasion. I wanted him to know I considered that he might be ok with the idea. I wasn't just randomly coming up with it right now.

Then, he pleaded, "I've done everything you've asked. I even..." and then the list of everything he'd done spilled out all over our Lobster. He went far beyond what he'd ever told me about before. He'd been keeping it all to himself. I was stunned.

Why didn't you tell me?

I guess you didn't want me to know?

Or maybe you did it for yourself?

Perhaps he thought it would change our marriage, and we'd reconnect.

I wish I had known.

By this point, there had been too much said and unsaid, too much done and undone in our unconscious marriage. We were just now becoming fully conscious of this. We'd been living two very different experiences in our relationship. Each of us reverted to our worlds to know ourselves, with visions of how we might reconnect. We were unclear how to find each other again. Still, my ever-positive hopefulness melted into one last possibility.

What if?

Shortly thereafter, we entertained the possibility of a conscious marriage. We took more risks and enjoyed our time together. We were freer and more playful as we opened up to new ideas. We didn't focus much on the past. We were living in the beauty of the here and now.

To celebrate our river city's 150th anniversary, we participated in its Venetian Boat Parade. I purchased and hung hundreds of solar lights across our luxury cruiser. At dusk, he captained us out onto the river behind a line-up of sailboats far more majestic with their tall, lighted masts. We flipped on our electric blue deck lights and floated like a blue spaceship. We stripped naked as we paraded in the fluorescent blue darkness. No one was the wiser. We giggled like children. It was so much fun.

It's funny how out in the dark waters, we became more comfortable together.

At some point during all the fun, the conversation shifted. He wondered, but didn't ask, if I'd slept with someone else. He watched my muteness intently. I was busy processing what I'd just heard. I'm sure he'd been planning his next comments all night long, waiting for the 'right' moment.

There was no right moment for this.

Out of nowhere, he named a fellow sailor and stated that if I had slept with him, he would be a good choice. He said he approved. I was shocked at what had just unfolded in front of me. It left me flabbergasted.

Was he opening up to the idea of an open marriage? Was he giving me his permission for it?

No way!

This could be the best of both worlds. We could stay married and openly enjoy intimacy, too!

A new dream for our marriage! A new conscious experience right in the present moment!

We could create our own set of rules within our new "we" space.

It was a brief new dream. That next weekend, when we went out on the water, he revealed his truth. He waited until he found some sort of comfortable moment, again. I was sunbathing while he daydreamed, looking out into the wind. His words floated over like an unassuming breeze. He'd been seeing someone else, and she wanted to be with him. He never dreamed he'd have another shot at a relationship with another woman. Just like that, he was out.

You've got to be kidding me.

What was last weekend all about, then?

Testing the waters?

One last hurrah?

I cried tears of disbelief. I never imagined our marriage would end. All the pivots of our relationship floated through my awareness. Consciously, I knew that this was where we were meant to be.

I was aware that calling 'this' a marriage was no longer the correct term. While it wasn't what I wanted, he said he was done. He'd made a different choice. One that I'd come to accept. I didn't want to be married to someone who didn't want to be married to me. I hadn't been home in months. Perhaps it was too much space for him.

When I finally returned home to gather my things, I noticed something different. On the very nail where he'd hung the first photo he'd taken of me was a new photo of some other woman tastefully posing in what used to be *our* bedroom. He obviously wanted me to notice.

I'd been replaced, in every meaning of the word.

I can't believe he hung her picture in the exact spot where I'd been hanging for the past eleven years.

Yes, he did. And I can't unsee that.

There is no turning back when the past is completed and the chapter ends.

In my growing conscious awareness, I walked down a new path into the unknown, where I found pure magic. Everything that had come before was my unconsciousness. It drained me to continue cycling it. When I intentionally unraveled it to let go of what no longer held value, I'd lost all desire for unconsciousness in any form. I'd changed my past, disconnected from the pull of its emotional turmoil, and transformed myself.

In the present, new possibilities flooded my awareness, and I could choose to create from them in exciting new ways. Suddenly, what was never on my radar became a new truth. My resilience aligned in every conscious, present moment. I'd found the magic of conscious living.

The surprising new truth was my conscious divorce. It contained more clarity than any other part of my eleven year relationship. It wasn't necessarily easy to transition from one version of my life story to another. Honestly, it wasn't that hard either. I'd rather I experience what I desire than remain stuck in time. I deserved my happiness just as he deserved his.

So when he started to point a finger on the last day of our agreement-making, I consciously shifted us to where I knew we were meant to be. I took us there.

"You're the one who started this," he shouted at me as if to burst my bubble." You said I would never be enough for you," he desperately cried out, triggering a barrage of now-empty grievances. His face was sad, and his words rigid and angry.

I sat still, calm, and centered as I expressed compassionate wisdom. Looking him in the eyes, I lifted the stake I'd plunged deeply between us, releasing us into sacred freedom. We'd come full circle into the center of our heads, each of us capable within our Rose-defined energy, living the separate lives we'd created for ourselves. I held softness in my heart for his final unconscious outburst.

"We are not doing it this way. It doesn't matter anymore who said what or who did what. The truth is, we've had two very different experiences of our unconscious marriage. Now, we're here, at this new point, forming agreements for our conscious divorce. That's what we are doing." My clear tones carried us back into our new conscious awareness as our past fell away.

I had already said he could have the house. I'd keep the boat since I was currently living on it. We didn't need two lawyers, I would coordinate our agreements. When he asked for more money, I agreed. When I asked him to leave my retirement fund untouched, he agreed. We walked our way through the conscious list. It didn't take long. It didn't cost much. The finality of it was rather uneventful, a 'meaningless' contract.

In our shared consciousness, we discovered unified agreements. We would each tell our families and circle of closest friends, and not speak poorly about the other. We wouldn't put people in the middle and ask them to choose between us. We'd let them know that even though we're divorcing, we're still friends. We're comfortable with our friends interacting with either one of us, both of us, or neither of us, for that matter. We'd allow others to be comfortable, without judgment.

The gentleness in our agreements spread further. We wanted to remain amicable. We would help each other out. We wanted to support each other in moving on. We'd compromise and be patient with each other. We'd support the best of everything for each other. In the end, we were finally creating our "we" space.

My story doesn't end here; it begins anew. As captain of my boat, I cruise into open waters and navigate the unknown with grace and wisdom. The freedom of the present blossoms into every possibility I dare to dream.

The moment that most closely embodies my sense of home is when my anchor sets and I'm completely untethered. The river holds me gently. The soothing harmony of nature reminds me I am not alone. Sunlight shimmers upon the water and in my heart.

In my floating stillness, I breathe—softened, peaceful, and buoyant. No longer pretending. No longer holding on. Only breath. Only home.

Michelle Wincell O'Leary is the Author of *Starlight: A Collection of Poems* inspired by her dreams during her twenties, which changed her life. In her new book, *Resilience: Flow in the Present* (2024), she adopts a higher, conscious writing style that opens the door to new possibilities for freedom in the present moment. (https://geni.us/FlowinthePresent)

Her journey into consciousness culminated in the Mastering Alchemy coursework, where she learned to transform her life and now serves as a Partner. She facilitates co-creative experiences with others to show how to harness their creative energies and reshape their reality.

Michelle holds a Master's degree in Counseling Psychology and is a licensed therapist in Minnesota, USA. She provides transformative support that has impacted countless individuals across the world, allowing them to navigate their journeys at their own pace, drawing on their innate wisdom. Her online energetic services are available worldwide.

Her extensive career in nonprofit health and housing has positively impacted thousands of lives, creating innovative, supportive environments for those facing health challenges and housing instability, while setting the standard for housing developments as healing.

Living aboard her boat on the Mississippi River, Michelle finds inspiration in nature, flowing with the current of life and following her conscious path.

As the creator of Spirit of Therapy, LLC, Michelle focuses on enhancing wellbeing for all. Through her course and personalized programs, Your Energy, Your Way, she fosters greater awareness in the present moment and encourages a deeper connection with consciousness. She also owns the Spirit of Therapy Publishing label and sells her books on her website, Amazon/Kindle, Apple Books, and other established book venues. Find more information at spiritoftherapyllc.net.

To explore her evolving insights, meditations, and creative tools, connect with her on Instagram and LinkedIn @michellewincelloleary and Facebook @maguireoleary. Find all of Michelle's links at Linktr.ee/michellewincelloleary.

FROM RUSSIA
WITH **LOVE**

By Olga Dewar

I thought it was over when I said, "I'm out!" Then I thought it was over when he moved out. But then I thought it was definitely over when I received a court document stating that we were officially divorced.

Now, I was sitting in a pew beside my son, listening to the remarks of some of his friends, and staring at the small cremation urn on the table of the steps to the altar. I was barely able to keep it together, and while going through an absurd amount of tissues, I suddenly realized that it was never over. I still loved him and always will.

This was a dark, painful moment. The pain of something unresolved. The pain of an unexpected loss. It felt like something was ripped right out of my soul and it left behind only a void. There are not enough words to describe it.

I think we all had questions on our mind. How could this have happened? Why didn't I do more to prevent this? What if I did not leave? Could we have worked it out? Could I have saved him?

Oh the pain! My soul was screaming, it was hurting. This was unbearable, and it was not just mine. This was the pain of our son, his parents, the extended family, his friends, and people who knew him. This was shocking and somewhat unexpected. This was a power of insurmountable collective pain.

But why was I so disturbed? After all, we were separated for over seven years. Why after some of the ugliest moments of our relationship and a breakdown of our marriage as a final blow, was I so disturbed by his sudden passing? Why do I still tear up every time I take myself back to that moment in the church?

It's best to start at the beginning.

THE BEGINNING

It was a cold, mid-September day in the early 1990s. I was at the giant open air arena Luzhniki. The air was filled with excitement as the grass field was disappearing under the feet of the crowd. More and more people were arriving, and at some point I was not sure how we all were going to fit here. The anticipation of what I was about to witness was overwhelming. Then it happened!

As the afternoon turned to an early evening, darkness descended over our huge gathering. It started to rain. My brand new T-shirt that I just purchased at the merch stand was soaked from the cold September rain. I nearly lost my voice from screaming and singing. I must have been shivering, but nothing could change the way I felt. I was at the first and only concert in Moscow of my biggest idol, Michael Jackson. But this was not the only reason I felt that my life was about to change.

This was our first date. I finally had a date with Michael, but there was someone else. He was also a foreigner who spoke English. MJ made it easy to have my first date with my future husband, and future father of my son.

I don't think either of us knew that at the time. We both found each other's company very pleasant. There seemed to be a real connection, and we did not hesitate to make it "official" after the concert.

When I think about our meeting, it might seem rather ordinary. He became a frequent figure at the bar that I was working at at the time.

My new boyfriend had a Russian friend who would come with him from time to time. The friend was tall, classically handsome, and very loud. He did not have any challenges chatting up the attractive young ladies. His broken English attracted a few foreign tourists and foreign staff that worked at the bar, and, of course, a few local Russian ladies who came in for a drink.

My future husband was different. He was attractive, tall, with strawberry blonde curly hair, and beautiful big blue eyes that carried a mystery. He was quiet and shy. Even when his friend encouraged him to speak, he had trouble. Although things got easier after a few drinks.

The more I got to know him, the more fascinated I was with him. Without any Russian cultural background, this amazing man learned the Russian language. It seemed that he knew more about Russian history than I did. He definitely saw more of the Soviet Union, including the Russian Federation, than I had. He was a BIG fan of Russia. So when we got together, it was not a surprise for him or his friends.

I was always attracted to accomplished men. I remember that in school my definition of the "high quality" boys was the fact that they did well in school and had great athletic abilities. As I started working, my attraction evolved. Now I was attracted to men with a drive, career, accomplishments, and once again had great athletic abilities. Perhaps this attraction was based on my own character. I was always driven, looking for more while keeping active.

However, as I found out later in life, appearances are not always what they seem to be, and love is blind! Cliche, I know. A great life lesson for anyone.

Yes, things were moving fast for us, because why not take action when things are fresh and exciting? Within a year, my staying over a couple of nights a week turned into me moving to his place. It was fun to play house, learning more about his "Canadian ways" and learning about his diet while discovering new-to-me foods.

One of the odd things at that time was peanut butter. This odd paste that tasted weird and felt weird in the mouth. "How can you possibly eat this crazy thing with a spoon? Yuck!" I commented several times, watching him enjoying a few spoonfuls of this strange concoction while we were watching TV on a couch.

Funny, it's been more than thirty years, and yet every time I pick up a jar of peanut butter now, I think of the first time I tried this (now) magical concoction.

Living together seemed like fun. We were both young adults. We both had jobs we liked. We were getting to know each other better. I had met a few of his friends. He knew most of mine already, since they all were part of Moscow's foreign crew (employees, patrons, and owners). He even met some of my former schoolmates. We were loving every moment of it.

We were truly enjoying life. I was learning more about Canada. I was learning his habits and his favorite dishes. I was understanding his likes and dislikes. It seemed rather easy, like a walk in a park. The more I paid attention, the more I learned. I wanted to be the "perfect" girlfriend and possibly a future wife. Yes, that thought crossed my mind a couple of times. It looked like I found THE ONE.

There was one thing that bothered me a little at first. He was drinking. We all were, but his drinking was different. He drank a lot and he was not always a happy drunk like myself or many of our friends. The alcohol seemed to bring some unpleasant behavior out in him. He would get angry about little things, or would start blaming the world for his problems. There was no taking responsibility even the day after. He was not violent or abusive, but such actions left an uneasy feeling.

The problem with drinking was that it was a curse on my family. Both of my grandfathers and my Dad were alcoholics. As a child, I lived through drunken scandals, verbal and physical abuse between my maternal grandparents and my parents. I worked through detaching myself from the times when I had to break up the physical fights of my grandparents, my mom and her father, and my own parents. Not a fun thing for a child.

The few drinks that he would have to loosen up usually turned into many more, and eventually created a problem. I should've seen it right from the beginning. I should've seen what it would create for us if the daily drinking continued.

But there was no possible way at the time, I was blindly in love.

Looking back, I realize that I was constantly finding excuses for his drinking and anger problems. The biggest excuse was him being away from his family in a completely different country. I kept convincing myself and others that he was a great guy, just under a lot of pressure. As you can imagine, eventually neither I nor others around him believed this bullshit. He was an addict.

I kept doing my thing, looking after everything and taking care of my man. I kept making fresh orange juice in the morning and cleaning his shoes in the evening. I was forgetting about myself and focusing on his needs. He seemed to be more important at the time. I wanted to make everything right for him. I wanted perfection and peace.

Amazing. As I write these words, I realize now that this relationship was doomed right from the beginning. I was "killing" myself to make someone happy. How could I have possibly thought that there would be some balance and respect that every relationship required when this relationship was one-sided? I loved him, but I did not love myself.

Things were getting serious between us, and we spoke more often about the possibility of marriage. It felt exciting and scary at the same time. We knew that if we got married, we'd be leaving Russia. The country was extremely unstable at the time and raising a family in Canada looked very welcoming.

We soon found out that we were expecting our first child. It was a surprise and not the most welcome one at that time. A month prior to the big news, I got really sick. I was running a very high fever, throwing up (that should have been suspicious), and I got so weak that I was unable to get out of bed. I visited a few specialists, yet it still was not clear what was wrong with me. There was an exorbitant amount of medication prescribed to make me feel better. Nothing seemed to work. I ended up in the hospital and had surgery with anesthesia, followed by a round of strong antibiotics within a day of admission. What was surprising was that there were no blood tests that could have shown that I was pregnant. There were no physical changes to my body that could have alerted me to the possibility of a pregnancy.

When the signs appeared within a couple of months, I was still under the observation of the surgeon. His first reaction was shock. "You cannot keep this baby!" he almost screamed. "There is a very high chance that your child will have mental or physical abnormalities. There is also a chance that the baby will not make it."

Shivers ran down my spine, I no longer heard anything else that the surgeon was saying. I felt sick, terrified, and angry. How could this happen? Why didn't the medical staff do what they were supposed to do before the surgery? What were we to do? This was my first pregnancy. Besides, prior to my illness, I was still having drinks and smoking. Oh my God! What have we done?

We both felt devastated. We were not ready for any of this. Making THE decision was the scariest part either of us had to encounter at that time. We were talking about a future human being, a fruit of our love.

There were a lot of tears. There were a lot of conversations. There was a lot of silence. There was a lot of separate time. There was a lot of thinking. And yes, there was a lot of drinking on his side. This was a sad time for our love. We were lost.

It took a long time to come to a decision, and by the time it was made, it was too late to interrupt the pregnancy, anyway. God made a decision for us. But that didn't really matter, we had decided to keep the baby and started focusing on a positive outcome.

We agreed not to share the news with anyone for now, especially our families. What would we tell them if we ourselves did not know what to expect at the end, if the baby would actually make it? We started making arrangements for a move since we still had a roommate. We also took more time to figure out what was next. We were considering a marriage, but the mood was off.

He started drinking even more. My friends who worked in bars noticed a difference in him. He was drinking more and getting angrier. I know it was not easy for him to keep such a heavy secret. To this day, I don't know exactly how he felt. All I knew was that he was not dealing with it well. At that time, I did not know how to help him. I was trying to figure things out as well, and I was the one carrying the baby. We were terrified of the future.

This was definitely not something I ever thought I would feel about the future. I always dreamed and planned. I always knew what I wanted and went after it. But now I felt empty. The "what ifs" were constantly with me. These were not my usual, exciting ""what ifs." Instead, they were: What if the baby does not make it? What if the baby makes it but has a disability? What if there is no baby, or the baby breaks us down? It was not easy. I could not share my fears with anyone, and he was not there to listen or share his thoughts. He was lost in a bottle.

The first few pregnancy appointments seemed to go well. The following few ultrasounds showed no abnormalities with the baby. This news made things easier and more hopeful.

He never attended those since he could not handle them well. Another excuse and avoidance of responsibility that I could not see at the time; It felt like I was dealing with it all alone. There was not much support. I voiced my concerns, and after a few conversations his behavior finally improved.

Time was passing by fast. I was handling a new job as I was getting bigger. Surprisingly, no one noticed the fact that I was pregnant. People simply thought that I gained a bit of weight. After all, I was small and with the right clothing, it was easy to hide my beautiful pregnant belly.

As the pregnancy kept progressing, I had yet to connect with the baby. It seemed strange, but I was not sure what to expect. Thinking about this now, I realize that no one actually knows the outcome. But at the time, this was not how I imagined my first pregnancy. Reflecting on that time now, I feel sad for the frightened young woman who did not know how to love herself or the baby that she was growing. Just now, as I write these words, I realized that I never forgave her. I never told her that I loved her. I never told her that she was strong, brave, and the most amazing and beautiful mama.

Tears! Yes, tears are rolling down my cheeks as I sit in my favorite coffee shop feeling this message through me, and channeling into all of you. Forgiveness is powerful! It does not matter when it comes. Love comes right after.

This is God's message and this time, he chose me to deliver it to you.

I was growing, and we had to start making decisions regarding the conversations we needed to have. My job was intense, I was on my feet 12-14 hours a day as an Assistant Manager of a popular, high-end, celebrity frequented, blues bar and restaurant. I could not continue doing it much longer. Our families did not have a clue, although as I found out later, my aunt suspected the pregnancy and shared that thought with my mom. My mom responded,

"She'd tell me if that was the case." Sadly, my mom was wrong in this situation.

We had to decide how we would support ourselves and the baby. I did not have maternity leave, which would mean that we would have to live on one salary and savings. This was where things started getting more unpleasant and real. I knew that his parents supported him financially. He received a certain amount a month. What I did not know was that he was not just putting it away in case he or we needed it in an emergency. After all, both of us got paid well. What I found out later, is that the money paid for drinking. It did not matter how many times we talked about becoming financially independent, he did not see it. He was comfortable with the crutch his parents provided for him.

That was not me. For as long as I could remember, I have had a drive for independence. That feeling of freedom to be yourself, to do what you love to do, to experience life in different ways. Money was something I enjoyed, always had, and could always find the way to make it. At the time, depending on someone for money felt uncomfortable and confined. The impending lack of money did not excite me.

We needed to make decisions. First to know was my job, since I was six months into my pregnancy and it was only fair to let my friend who was the manager and the owners know that I would be leaving in a few months. Then, we found out that the parents of my partner and their friends planned a trip to Russia for educational purposes, and to meet my family. They knew their son was serious about "some Russian girl." I remember thinking, how *dare* they call me "some girl!" Just kidding, of course. This was BIG!!!

Due to all this pressure, his alcohol intake and the tension at home were getting unbearable. I was keeping it together by once again relying on making excuses for him. All of my friends thought I was crazy and encouraged me to break the relationship off. They had yet to know what we were expecting.

One of the most shocking situations was when one of the owners of the business I worked at proclaimed his love for me. He knew I was in a committed relationship and by then, he knew that I was having a baby. He did not care! He felt disgusted by the way my partner treated me. He thought I deserved so much more, and most importantly, he thought I deserved more love and respect. He kept pursuing me and I have to say, it felt so good to be cared for. Things were not well at home, and this was a bright light in my dark world back then.

I recall having a conversation with my friend about this man. They knew each other better since my friend was invited by the three owners to help them open the place. They could not think of anyone better than me to help him do that, so I became part of the "family." My friend shared more with me about this man, and he even encouraged me to consider the possibility. My friend, who also knew my partner, was also not thrilled with the way I was being treated, especially now that I was pregnant.

I found the man very attractive, caring, and respectful; and yes, the temptation was high. He tried to be present at work every day at least for a few hours to make sure I was okay. He always brought me flowers, he made sure I ate, and tried to help with any other responsibilities that came with running the restaurant, even if it was just for an hour or so. He tried really hard. He was married once and had an adorable daughter from that marriage. He checked all the boxes for me. The problem was, I was in love. Even through the toughest times for myself (and the baby at that time), I was concerned with how the separation would affect my partner. "It will kill him!" I used to tell my friend. "I could not forgive myself for hurting him!"

And so I continued. It was like swimming against the current. I truly believed and convinced everyone around me (or at least I thought I did) that he would change when the baby was born. "It's just the fear of the unknown, he'll turn it around," I kept saying to myself and to everyone we knew.

One of my superpowers, I never give up.

As long as I can remember, I've loved dreaming. Well, what child doesn't? Looking back now, I realize that I almost always got what I dreamed about. Why? I had the drive, and I just knew that as long as I kept dreaming, things would work out. So why give up? Some people from my past would question this statement, after all, there are many things I had "given up." But my dearest, letting go is not giving up. You have to know when it's time.

Time was ticking, his parents were coming, What were we to do? We were not sure. There were no instructions for this situation. We decided just to roll with it. He told me that he would find the time to speak to his parents about our situation. I trusted him with that big secret. My family still did not have a clue, all they knew was that there was a foreign family coming over to meet them and they had to be on their best behavior.

September came fast, and we were faced with his family's visit and decisions. He chose not to tell his family anything about the pregnancy while they were in Russia. He decided not to spoil their experience. I somewhat agreed. It was not my decision, and this was not my family. They did not find out till the day I went to the hospital for delivery. I could not understand why he decided to wait that long. Just now I realize, he must have felt like a small child who had done something wrong. He still had to grow up.

My family found out a few weeks after the Canadian family visit. My Mom was very pleased. As I found out later, my Dad was also very excited, though at the time, he was out of the country. It felt great to finally let the BIG secret out. I was young, but I felt ready, perhaps because I already played the role of "mom" to my younger brother at ten years old.

At the end of the day, none of that really mattered. His family had a great visit. They thought I was "chubby" without knowing the main reason, and we had a great time getting to know each other. We had many laughs, and got together with my extended family at my grandma's place and then spent some intimate time in St. Petersburg. The families seemed different at first, but at the end of the day, we all seemed as one.

A few months passed by and the BIG delivery day was at our doors. It was one of those days that we prepared for for a long time but still were not ready for. It just arrived. I woke up one day and said, "Today is the day." I did not know how it was supposed to feel. I just knew the baby was arriving. As we got to the hospital, the doctors confirmed that I was close to delivering a baby. This was great news since I carried it to term, even a little over.

On the date of the scheduled delivery we were at the Danish embassy celebrating something with our international friends. Everyone came to me asking when the baby was due. Well, the baby was due on that day and there was no indication that it was happening. Many jokes were made that if the baby came along during my stay at the embassy, the baby could have Danish citizenship. At that time we were open to anything.

The baby decided to make its appearance ten days after the due date, on December 12, 1994. He decided to announce the baby's attempt early in the morning so his parents could finally make some decisions. My parents knew, his parents still did not know. He called them after delivering me to the hospital. He waited till the last possible minute. Of course, they were shocked, but they were also excited to become grandparents for the first time. They were well into their 60s, it was the right time even though they were not expecting it.

The birth was tough, Dad was not allowed in the delivery room at the time, and then my baby was taken away from me because he did not cry "right." It took me a couple of days to come to myself and realize that I had not seen the baby since the birth. I spoke to the nurse, and she advised that the baby and I needed some alone time, and that I could visit the baby at any time. I realized that once again, I was alone. Though I had great care staff around me, they were strangers. They did not know me. They did not know my situation.

There were complications so it took over ten days for the baby and I to get out of the hospital. While in the hospital, my partner stood up to the challenge. He delivered everything that I requested. He visited almost every day while seeing the baby only as a little speck through the window of the fourth story. On one cold snowy December day, he drew an "I love you!" sign in the snow for me and our son. It was very romantic. His notes indicated that he could not wait to see us at home. I was hopeful. I felt that maybe things would be different, and he was finally showing me that he was capable of more.

I was excited about his enthusiasm. He seemed like a new man. Despite the doctor's suggestions, I begged them to let me go home. I eventually convinced them that I would receive proper care at home. Boy, was I wrong.

The day of the release finally came, and I was ecstatic to share this beautiful child with his Dad. After all the worries, the baby turned out to be perfectly fine with some minor muscle tension issues. There were no visible physical abnormalities. We were happy. All we had to watch for now were his mental capabilities.

We were first-time parents. We were blessed and this was the first grandchild for both sets of our parents. Our son was the first great-grandchild for my grandmother, and he was also a first nephew for his Dad's sister and some of my cousins. This little guy had a lot of love around him and many interested parties in his upbringing.

Our son was developing well and was ahead of the chart of growth. His mental development was also on track, so we were very pleased once again. We had decided that it was best for our little family to move to Canada. This move would provide more stability and better opportunities for all of us. In order to arrange this move, it was best for us to get married. At this point, we did not have a doubt that we'd continue growing together as a couple and now as a family. These were very exciting times.

I thought that the days with our newborn would reduce stress for my partner. Things were falling into place and we were getting ready for a move. Yes, there were copious amounts of things to do, but all of them led to the possibility of a better life for all of us.

My enthusiasm was not met. After my release from the hospital, he was around more for about a week. Then, he would barely be at home. After work, he would go to a bar and stay out till the early hours of the morning. At the time, there were no cell phones. I did not know where he was or what he was up to. I didn't know if he was dead or alive. He was still a foreigner in Russia and the times were turbulent. He got mugged once at the entrance of our old apartment building. This was not helping the baby or me.

My friends would encourage him to go home. Some started refusing to serve him after a certain hour or after a certain amount of drinks. Then some stopped running a tab for him. They could not understand how he could be out every day till very late into the night or morning while he had a new baby at home. His excuse was, "I don't know what I am doing. I am scared to hurt the baby." *Are you fucking kidding me?*

What did that even mean? What about me? Did he think that as a woman I had an instruction book about baby care built into my brain? That I had a Master's in raising a human being? That I was not scared, worried, frustrated, and exhausted? My body just had gone through a HUGE transition within the last nine months. Nevermind my brain. WTF!

Now we also had financial challenges since most of the money was going to drinking. My family was helping with what they could. They were getting frustrated with the situation as well. They talked to him, begged him to be reasonable, and tried to support him mentally in any way they knew how. I had many stern conversations with him about the support from his parents. I did not want them to send him money every month because they did not have a clue what the money was going for.

Many years later, after his death, while cleaning some boxes with his documents, I found a large folder of faxes (yes, this was the fastest way to communicate back then). They included letters with pages and pages of excuses why he needed more and more money. I realize now that I had no idea how much money was going through his hands. It's very sad considering we did not live well, we struggled.

Yet, through all the tears, stress, fights, and arguments, I still stayed with him. At this point, I could not see myself separating him from the baby. I was focused on us leaving Russia with great hope that when we got to Canada, things would stabilize and we would be happy. I truly thought that with less stress and discomfort, he would turn his life around. I was focused! Once again, I was not about to give up.

There was one positive change in him. When he was with our son, he was protective and caring. As the baby got older and could interact more, his Dad got more involved. I remember one particular situation that pleasantly surprised me. Growing up in my maternal grandparents' home, there were always animals. It seemed that my partner also grew up with cats in the home. During one of the visits by our little new family to my grandmother, our son got really interested in grandmother's cat. The cat was a mature male and he had not met any babies. Our son was about five months old at the time and was able to sit and reach for things by now. Of course, when the cat decided to make himself comfortable against the large pillow that was supporting the baby sitting, our son's curiosity took over. His head turned, he tilted, and his little hand grabbed the cat's fur. As you can imagine, the cat was not impressed. He hissed and whacked the baby with his paw. What happened next astounded everyone present. My partner, who really loved this cat, jumped off the couch, grabbed the cat by the scruff, shook and screamed at the cat, and threw him out of the room. There was a temporary silence. I don't think anyone was expecting such a strong reaction from this usually quiet and balanced guy. This was the moment that I understood how much he cared about our little son.

The months were moving fast. We got married, got our paperwork completed, and purchased the tickets for Canada. Things were getting more exciting. There was a different life waiting for us across the ocean. All I could see was peace and love in our family. No more fighting, struggling, and begging for a change. To me, this move was the light at the end of the tunnel.

THE MIDDLE

As we boarded the airplane with our eight-month-old son, I felt relieved. We were together on the way to the new way of living. We flew through Amsterdam and decided to stay there for a night. It was a great opportunity for me to see the city and have a bit of a reprieve for the baby before the very long flight across the ocean. It seemed like a great idea. I loved the drive from the airport. This was a new world for me. The old streets of Amsterdam, the endless green fields, and, of course, the windmills. I felt that I was transported into a book or onto a movie set. There were so many new and exciting things around me. One thing however, did not change. After arriving at the hotel, my partner suggested that he go out and get us something to eat. I considered going with him, but I was tired just like our little guy. So, he went on his own and did not come back for several hours. Just like that, leaving his hungry wife and little son alone. He came back with cold food, buzzed from alcohol and grass. To this day, I do not understand what was going through his head. Of course, I thought something bad happened to him.

The next day we were on the way to Canada. In my mind, we were so much closer to that missing link. On a hot summer August day we landed in Ottawa. His parents were there to meet us. They were the last ones to know we were expecting. Now, they could not wait to meet their first grandbaby.

We arrived! The drive to our new home was beautiful. To start, we were going to live with my husband's parents. They had a lovely four bedroom home and were very kind to help us settle and get on our feet. My husband's room was turned into the baby's room and we got a large bedroom that was formerly a library while only grandparents had been living there.

It took a few days to get used to the time change, after all the time difference between Ottawa and Moscow was eight hours. Then it took another few weeks to meet various relatives, curious friends and neighbors and for our son and me to meet our new doctor. Life was flowing brilliantly.

My husband decided to go back to school to upgrade his tech skills since he had been out of the country for a few years. Technology was starting to boom and the area we lived in was perfect for a knowledgeable IT person. The plan for me was to stay home with the baby, get acclimated to Canadian culture, and improve my English. Life was good.

We got into the routine of living in Canada. Things between us got better. He was at home more, helping with the baby while helping me to learn more about the world we lived in now. There were occasional dates with his friends, but nothing seemed to be that bad.

I also realized that alcohol was part of this family's everyday life. No, they were not drinking to get drunk, they simply enjoyed a cocktail before dinner and a glass of wine with dinner. I enjoyed doing the same, but noticed that my husband would often have another cocktail before or after dinner. It was part of his life for so long that I could understand the need for it. But now I could see this was not going to go away.

I tried speaking with my husband's Dad since he was the one still providing him with money. I explained to him that money did not go to where it's needed, rather it was spent without thought. He responded that would be more careful and would ask for reasoning when his son approached him with a request for money again. I was new to the family, and it must have been difficult for my father-in-law to understand why I was getting involved in their decisions. I came from a tight-knit family where everyone seemed to know everyone's business. I am sure my request made my father-in-law feel uncomfortable at the time.

Life continued as it did. The living conditions were much better than in Russia. I was more occupied trying to figure out what was next for me. Our son was now over two years old, and I was itching to go back to work and have my own income. I really did not enjoy being dependent on someone else for money. After a discussion with the family, it seemed like part-time work was a good start. I did not have a clue what it would look like.

After trying a few places, I quickly understood that my previous experience did not fit well in the new area we lived in. Ottawa was a HUGE downgrade in size from Moscow. I realized that if I wanted something more sustainable and professional, I had to go back to school. Also, the hours of my work did not work well with my husband. We barely had any time to see each other.

By that time, we moved to our own place and we no longer had almost daily support of my in-laws. They lived close, but had a very active lifestyle, so my husband and I worked together to make sure our son had great care. We loved our little house and quickly settled into a new family life. It seemed all was going well, but we hit a wall once again. My husband was not coming home right after work anymore. Most of the time he'd stop by the local pub for a drink or two "to chill" before coming home. There was one dish that I used to make that almost guaranteed a disagreement. It was fried steak with mushrooms, onions, and usually mashed potatoes. The first couple of times when I made it, we had an argument. Then I noticed that every time I made it and waited for him to come home after work, he never did. He was always late. My son and I always waited for him, until one day I said, "Fuck it! We're not waiting for Dad." From then on, I did not make it unless he was home.

Once again the fights and arguments became frequent. All of them were related to his lack of anger management and drinking, which in turn exacerbated his anger problem. It was a vicious loop. I tried talking to him. I tried loving him more. I tried begging him. I once again reached out to his parents, since now they were out of the everyday loop. I reached out to a couple of his friends asking for a suggestion and got reprimanded after for sharing our private life. Nothing seemed to work. There was no acknowledgment of the problems that he had. It always was someone else's fault; someone made him mad, someone made him angry, someone stressed him out. None of it was on him. NOT. A. SINGLE. THING. I was at the end of my rope.

The last straw for me was the change in our son. At that time he was attending nursery school and was a happy, curious, little guy. With the decline of a positive atmosphere at home, I'd noticed a change in him. He was becoming frustrated, angry, and unhappy. He was more nervous and sad. My heart broke! I suddenly saw some pieces of my childhood that I would not want my son to have. I realized that the situation between my husband and me needed to be resolved. Unfortunately, he did not hear, listen, or observe any of the changes. So, one day, I woke up, and I knew that part of my soul dedicated to my husband had died. This was the end. I had nothing left to offer him.

I carried this scary feeling inside for several months. I did not know what to do, but I also knew that we couldn't continue like this. I suddenly realized that I completely lost myself with him. I gave him all I could and he simply drained me. Somewhere deep in my heart, I knew I still loved him, but it was so deep that every time I saw him now, I had a feeling of disgust. How could you possibly live like that while raising a little human? Sure you could hide it, but children feel your truth.

He knew something was amiss. I got more quiet. I stopped arguing and stopped really caring about him or his behavior. I stopped paying attention to him. Of course, he did not like it. But what can you ask from a "dead" person? I remember one day waking up and making a decision that I could no longer be with this man. The biggest thing was that I could not see our son suffer anymore. He was still young, just a few months short of four. To me, this was the best time for us to separate. If we waited any longer, our boy would suffer even more. I knew this would not be taken well and had to prepare myself for the conversation mentally.

It was October of 1998. We had just celebrated Thanksgiving with the extended family, and were getting close to celebrating a year in our new home. I agreed to host a Halloween party at our house with his friends, as I'd yet to have any of my own. This was an easy transition I thought, something to occupy my mind. Everyone had a good time. I played a great hostess focusing on our son and the guests. A couple of people stayed over and went for a walk the next morning. This detail escapes me now, but I believe that my husband came back from a walk earlier while his sister took some extra time with our son at a playground.

He once again had a lot to drink the night before and I am sure did not feel that well. I didn't notice and at this point did not care. When he came in and settled, I told him that we needed to talk. He joked, "Oh, it's one of those...." I said,"Yes, it is. I am out!" He sat there with a lost gaze in his eyes. "What do you mean, you're out?" he asked with a nervous tone. My response was calm and polished, "I am exhausted and don't want to do this anymore." Silence. I was ready for what came next.

His face got red, his eyes flashed, his breath became rapid. He was taken by surprise and I could see how angry he was getting. I stayed calm, although inside I was getting ready for a fight. What followed included screaming, accusations, and angry outbursts. He was in shock. Of course, he did not see it coming. In his eyes, everything was wonderful and fantastic. I stayed calm with a ready answer to every question. I was not reacting to any of the nonsense that flew my way. He was asking if there is any way to fix the situation and I advised him that I've tried for many years and I simply have nothing left to offer. Of course, once again he suggested that he did not know that things were this bad. I had many responses to that one, but I chose to bring up none. What was the point?

After some time, he got up and left the house. He left with a bang, literally, by slamming the front door shut. I was curious where he went but did not really care. I suspected that he went to his parent's place, which I found out later. When our son returned home, he was asking about his Daddy and I had to explain that Daddy had to go to his parents' house to help them (at the time I didn't even know that). This was the first lie of many that I told our son about his Dad and his behavior. I did not feel well. I felt rotten.

Here I was still making excuses for this man, now to our son. Gosh, just now I realized that his Dad had trouble growing up. This was the moment I realized that he was not ready for the responsibilities of the family. Yes, our son arrived unexpectedly, but we seemed to be very excited about starting a family together. I remember a tender moment of one night when it was his "turn" to be with the baby, he proudly told me with tears in his eyes, "I never thought I'd be a father." I knew my decision was hurting him badly.

THE END

It happened, now what? Well, this was just the start of an unknown. All I knew was that I started a change. A change for myself, a change for our son, and a change for my husband. I didn't even expect what was coming next.

After about a week of struggle, my husband decided it was a good idea to stay with his parents for a while. I knew it was not easy for him. It wasn't easy for anyone. It was very challenging to keep finding excuses for our son while Daddy was not staying home. It was a very painful time for all of us. We were all struggling.

Through distance, he decided it was time to step up to the plate and treat me better. Along came the gifts, the flowers, and the dinners out. Unfortunately, it was a little late. I still felt dead inside. I felt not one bit of love for him any longer. I tried hard and was as appreciative as I could be of the gestures. But I simply checked out. I did not see a way forward. Clearly, the response he was getting from me was not what he was hoping for. "I want everything or nothing!" he screamed when he didn't get his way. What? Was this the tactic to get me back? This was not helping our already injured relationship.

We were getting nowhere. His parents got involved. We all tried to figure it out. He even finally suggested marriage counseling, a method that I hoped we would use back when I was still "alive." We tried. It was not helping.

Then came (what we thought was) the BIG decision. After many conversations and negotiations, we decided to give it another shot. We did not do it for us, we did it for our son. We decided to go on a family trip for a week or so.

What were we thinking? This was a BIG mistake! I had to keep it together. I tried to make it as enjoyable for all of us as I could.

But It was not working. We both knew it. When we got back home, we understood that we were done. The last possible chance for reconciliations did not work. It was time for us to go our separate ways. It was very painful to watch our little guy trying to figure out why Mummy and Daddy did not like each other very much anymore.

Living separately brought peace, at least at first. He was angry. He was not willing to forgive or understand why I did this to our little family. Then came the crazy drunk voicemail rants. Then angry emails with threats. I remember one day he popped by the house to pick something up. We got into an argument. We were standing very close to each other. This is when he looked at me with mad eyes and punched the wall right beside me. This was the first time I felt threatened. I felt that he would never move on.

His work suffered, and so did his health. Mental and physical. It seemed like every time I saw him, he was 'disappearing.' He was not coping well. I started feeling guilty and wondered if there was anything I could do to help him to get through this. My invitations only created more animosity. He would refuse to see his son from time to time. I was angry at him about it. I did not understand why he would punish our son.

It lasted for years, and suddenly things quieted down. He understood that I was not coming back. He understood that it was important for him and our son to repair their relationship. So it seemed like he took steps. He did his best to live and enjoy his life. He and our son went on some road trips. He took more interest in our son's school and started attending more hockey games.

By then, our son was old enough and knew how to manage his parents. I was bad at asking him not to share certain things with his Dad. He on the other hand, as I found out later, was not sharing some things with me about his Dad. At the time, I was happy that they were rebuilding, even though most of the time the homework was not done after the weekend visits.

This connection between them reminded me why I loved my husband. After all the things we went through, he was still a guy who loved his son, who was still an intelligent person, and a man who helped our son and me to have better opportunities. I still loved him, even if it was not a romantic love.

Then the inevitable. A rough few years of the death of his cat, friends, and unexpected death of his Mom and my Dad within two weeks of each other, all played a role in him falling further into his life of despair. Years of unemployment and an unhealthy lifestyle were killing his mind and body. The last time I saw him was at our son's hockey game. He looked extremely bloated, the whites of his eyes and skin were yellow. He had cracked lips and awful yellow teeth. He looked like a man who completely gave up on himself. I had not seen him in a while and his appearance shocked me. He was only forty!

My father-in-law attended the game as well, and I made a point of speaking with him and begging him to take his son to the hospital. He agreed that it was time and they'll have a conversation. Conversation? It was out of my hands. All I could do was pray and hope for the best.

A few days later, our son had an event at school and asked Dad to attend it. The next day, school had a PD day and our son was to spend it at the friend's house. I was at work. Then my desk phone rang, it was my father-in-law. I could not understand what he was telling me. I kept asking, "What do you mean?" His son, my son's Dad, and my ex-husband were gone. He was no longer living.

I do not recall much after that. Shortly after the call, I found myself in the car, in tears, driving to pick up our son from his friend to share the news. "How am I going to tell him this?" was all I could think of. I finally called my son and told him I was on my way to pick him up. He was very displeased and asked me why. I advised that I'd let him know when I got there and that it was important. I did my best not to cry when I spoke with him.

What came next was the toughest thing I had to do with my son yet. He came out to the car, he knew something was off. I asked him to get in and close the door. I gathered myself. "Hunny, I am really sorry, but your Dad passed away." Momentary silence. I was not expecting to hear the following. In a shocked and frustrated manner our son slapped his palms on his thighs and screamed, "I knew it! I knew it! I knew this was going to happen!" Then he started crying. I was confused by what he said, but that did not matter at the time. All I wanted to do is to make him feel better and for his Dad to be alive.

These were very tough times. We were still recovering from the sudden death of my Dad and my mother-in-law just seven months prior. I could not imagine what my father-in-law and my sister-in-law must have felt. This was unimaginable. It hurt so much. It hurt more because our baby was affected and I did not know how to make it better.

The saddest part was that my husband's family was expecting that something unpleasant would happen soon. They expected a hospital stay and perhaps a trip to rehab. I don't think anyone expected this. This was an extreme outcome of his lack of care for his well being. At some point, he gave up. Sadly, all the members of the family, including our son knew it. As events and conversation were progressing, I found out that his Dad was not well for a while and was trying to turn his life around. He was doing it on his own, without any support. Unfortunately, his body was so sick that it needed medical intervention. He was too late.

I also understood that our son was protecting his Dad. This poor kid thought that if he shared with anyone the way his Dad lived, he'd get him in trouble. He was doing this for several years. Oh, the pressure and the damage in later years. He did what he thought was the right thing at the time. I don't think anyone could have made any difference, all was up to his Dad. Sadly, his Dad was already too far gone well before his ultimate demise.

All the dreams and plans of the two men, one only thirteen and the other one only forty-one, were now shattered. "Mom, he was my best friend!" my son told me during those very tough days. They had just rebuilt their relationship and started having a lot more fun together. His Dad introduced him to F1, one thing that we now enjoy together. He introduced our son to video games, which I still do not play. He introduced our son to classic rock, just as he introduced me to some of the best rock bands when we just met. He brought so much light into our lives. He brought humor, fun, intelligence, and adventures. He was loved by all till the end of his days. Sadly, he did not seem to love himself.

All the hurt, pain, and suffering that we went through just kept reminding me that they were temporary. Love was always there. Love was always among us. What I understood on that day in church is that you can find the most beautiful love in some of the ugliest places. I also understood that LOVE was my SUPERPOWER.

Growing up in the Soviet Union, Olga was always striving for more—more knowledge and recognition as a child, and a better, more prosperous life as an adult. She seemed to know from the early days that she was destined for something bigger. She lived in her imagination and conquered the world with overachievements in grades, athletics, and extracurricular activities.

It all changed in September of 1992. Life shifted, and so did Olga's perspective on it. The birth of her son in 1994, and a big move across the Atlantic Ocean in 1995, opened a new world that Olga dreamt about. It was not quite what she imagined it to be, but the life experiences brought her exactly what she was searching for: new perspectives, an open mind, spiritual growth, and beautiful self-discovery.

Now, as a bestselling author and a Personal Growth Mentor, she guides others to find more happiness in their everyday lives and encourages them to see it from a different perspective. If you like to find out more, you can visit happinessbyyou.com or follow her on Instagram @olgadewar.

5

OTHER SIDE OF THE BOTTLE

By Lauren Baca

"I don't want to be married anymore!" I said to a perfect stranger.

Across from me, lying on a white faux fur rug in the book corner, was a blonde-haired, blue-eyed beauty snuggled into her grey fuzzy North Face jacket and black sweats. We had been sitting in the corner of our boys' Montessori classroom for what felt like hours while they prepped for the children's school photos. We sat commiserating about life, parenthood and marriage. I had never spoken such candid words to anyone, not even myself! There was something about her, what she said and how she said it, or maybe it was what she didn't say that for the first time maybe ever allowed me to speak my truth without judgment. I couldn't believe myself! How could I say that to this woman I was going to see every day at school? I don't recall her exact response, but I do recall the conversation being seamless, and non judgmental. Elizabeth later became my best friend.

I spent years, almost a decade, denying my inner voice, my intuition. Fighting myself to the end, thinking that I needed to be something more for him. I thought that if I loved him enough, if I could get him to see this beautiful life we had created, if I could be more of what he needed me to be, that I could find a way to make it work. I wanted to make him love me more, not just for me, but for our kids. But no matter how much I shape shifted into different versions of myself to fit into the box of our marriage, was he going to change?

The multiple moves across cities, to a new state and then to different cities in a new state were never enough! And I was exhausted! Exhausted from the never ending search for something different—a new job, a new city, a new home. The list was endless. And it wasn't just a list of goals, it always felt like whatever the "it" thing was, we had to be on the hunt for it. We had to make a change of some sort, like the filling of an empty void. The shopaholic mindlessly spends money to fill the empty space in their heart (and maybe because they love to shop).

I remember we had listed our home on the market for a second time in a whirlwind; we cleared closets, prepped the house for listing photos and open houses, all so we could make yet another move! It was exhausting! This time further away from city life, from anyone we knew. I didn't want to do it. I didn't care how much bigger our house could be, or that we could have chickens if we wanted and land that we weren't going to be spending an exorbitant amount of time on. Deep in my heart I was done making concessions, not just for me, but more importantly for our kids.

Our kids were still very young, but started to establish themselves within their elementary school, finding their tribes and feeling good about their surroundings. And I finally made mom friends of my own, establishing our new found adult life in this beautiful, coveted neighborhood and city, and I didn't want to go! We had moved from California to Texas, and in the short time we had lived in Texas, we had already moved our family three times, to three vastly different cities. First was near my mom in a rental. Then, we "had" to buy a house (honestly, I was fine with the rental near my mom), so we bought a darling little house in a tiny town forty-five minutes east of city life and twenty minutes away from any amenities or anything convenient. After a year or two of living too far out in the country, we decided to make another shift, this time to the town we had hoped to move to when we originally came to Texas. So when my ex said he wanted to move yet again, my stomach churned. Not only would this be another relocation, it was way out in the middle of nowhere, *again*! Far away from, well, everything. And in our town at the time, everything was 5-8 minutes away. You could literally drop off your kids at school, do your Target pick up, go through the car wash and be home in less than thirty-five minutes if you did it right!

My ex had a way of talking me into things by just talking about them until I didn't want to discuss them anymore. He would wear me down until it felt like the only way to make it stop was to just agree. "Okay, you want to move, let's make that happen. You want to plant trees in the yard, redesign the front of the house, move again, build a house... buy a new truck...," whatever the fixation became, it was like I became a "yes" girl, all in the name of peace. Every concession was made to make the conversation stop and end the noise in my head, even when many of the times I didn't agree. I was in a constant battle with myself, silently imagining what I wanted to say to my ex, but just never being able to.

Among the chaos of listing our house for sale, we went out to celebrate our anniversary by going to see the Florida Georgia Line at an outdoor venue here in Texas. It was late spring, the air was hot and dewy, filled with humidity. The music was loud and filled my heart space, behind us the stars shone bright and the state fair ferris wheel lit up the skyline. Tears flooded my eyes, as they sang "H.O.L.Y." I knew at that moment we couldn't move! I wasn't going to move! I wasn't going to move our family. When we got home I took a long hot shower, closed my eyes, and prepared myself saying, "You can do this." As soon as I stepped out of the shower, I walked down the hall to the family room, still wet and wrapped in my navy towel, my ex sitting on the sofa comfy and relaxed. I blurted out, "We're pulling the house off the market, I don't want to move, we're not doing this!"

. . .

Someone gave me a magnet when I was in my 20s—it read, "Listen to the compass of your heart, all you need lies within." It was a gift I received in college after I broke off my engagement, packed up my things while my fiancé was at work, and moved out of the very lovely home he was building for us, deciding to go back to school.

I've kept that magnet on my fridge since my college days.

I couldn't tell you who gave it to me, but I can tell you those are words to live by, even now in my 40s. But was I truly living by it? As I stand in my partner's home, watching the kids play outside as I make dinner, I realize even now, I am not living this quote in any way. "All I need lies within." The truth sets you free, your voice sets you free, your intuition sets you free! Freedom. Peace. That's what I wanted most. I was seeking peace, not because we fought all the time, but peace in my mind. A peace that would make all that chatter go away, stop the fighting in my head, and the constant justifications as to why I was still in my marriage. Freedom from the constant questioning of myself as to why I couldn't make our marriage work, or why I couldn't find a way to make him stop drinking. I wanted to release it all, knowing it no longer served me.

The days leading up to me exploding my life, I had a chemical peel facial. Two babies, a lot of hormones, and Melasma spots on my face had sent me into a tailspin for far too long. Prior to the birth of my daughter, my skin was like porcelain; post my daughter's birth I felt like I had sat in the sun my whole life, and had the sun damage of an unkept older woman. Call it conceded if you will, but we all have that one thing that really bothers us about ourselves; for me, it was the dark spots on my face. So, in an effort to make myself feel better about my life slowly unraveling (and better about myself in general), I had a chemical peel. Now, if you know anything about chemical peels (and if you don't, I'll tell you the short of it), your face basically falls off! And when I say my face was falling off, I mean literally sheets of skin were peeling off my face, around my mouth, at the tip of my nostrils, all cracking and peeling. There was nothing cute about it. Fast forward to a few days post my peel. My face was red and hot like fresh, first summer sunburn falling off, and my inner chatter was at the highest volume for weeks leading up to the implosion.

I can't do this

What will I do...?

What will I say?

How do I even do this, say this... I'm about to blow up my kids' lives!

Can they handle this? Can I handle this?

Can I help them handle this?

Is this the right decision?

I've made it this far. Maybe I can wait it out just a bit longer, hold on for a bit longer, something will change.

Or maybe if I do leave him something will change, he'll see, he'll want to change, he'll want to make it work!

But I'm so mad at him. I'm always doing everything alone, I'm alone all the time, I may as well be alone if I'm basically doing all the things alone, so really what's the difference?

Just writing this makes me tired. It is no wonder I felt burnt out from my life. I wasn't living, I was barely surviving.

It was later in the evening when I blew up my life, looking the most unattractive I have ever looked or felt. Typically, if you're breaking up with someone, you at least want to look good—I looked downright frightful (looking back, it's kinda funny). My face falling off, ratty gray joggers and a T-shirt, bare feet—every step on our dark hardwood floor, down the hallway to the backroom felt like another bomb exploding as I made my way to the finale of an explosion. My heart beat so hard and so fast I could feel my pulse through every limb of my body; I turned the long silver sideways handle on the backroom door, opened it swiftly, the exhilaration coursing through my veins.

"I want you to move out of the house. I'm done. I want you out!"

BOOM. Imagine a hurricane meeting a tornado, meeting a nuclear bomb level of explosiveness. That's how that moment felt!

My voice was stern and serious, my eyes laser-focused on my husband who sat in the nearly empty room, hiding from our life and drowning out the world in whatever Netflix show he was watching. My facade fell off and revealed a nasty look of disdain and disgust. My heart was pounding, leaving a feeling of deep, uncontrollable grief and sadness. My mind went blank except to tell myself, "You did it Lauren. You just blew up your life. You set this next series of events into motion, and there is NO going back now, I'm proud of you!" Ironically, after telling him to move out, I left the house pretty quickly after and went straight to my best friend's house.

I jumped in my car with tears pouring down my face, inconsolable, sobbing, and candidly close to hysterical. I made it to the front of her house where she stood waiting. I got out of the car and melted into her warm, loving hug that only a best friend can give you.

"I blew up my life!" I blubbered.

"You're going to be okay, friend..." she whispered as she hugged me tight, "You're going to be okay... and I'm going to be here for you through it all."

I went home that night and slept in the guest room. The air felt colder and crisper in there, and suddenly I felt like the walls of our house were caving in on me, dark, sad, and weeping at what was happening within their confines. I laid there, curled up, wondering what was to come next for me, for us. I was in uncharted waters, and that alone gave me more anxiety than I knew what to do with.

I turned on the large TV and turned on *Sleepless in Seattle* for familiar faces, voices, and a happy story, eventually drifting off to sleep. When I awoke I thought, *I made it through the first real rough, anxiety ridden night of many to follow.* I knew I needed to find a way to manage it, otherwise the fear of the unknown, of how my life was about to unfold was going to eat me alive. That was the start of my running journey: of reading, journaling, meditation, and turning to something greater than myself. That's where I started to find peace and healing.

· · ·

My ex would refer to me as a shapeshifter, negative and unpredictable. "One minute you're fun... the next, not so much." I am what I would describe as an introverted social butterfly, with capabilities that span from being the life of the party, being part of the party, and then being a wallflower, silent and gone quickly like a butterfly that floated by. You blinked and it was gone! "Shape shifting" was one of my coping mechanisms, self-taught at a young age perhaps; my own personal survival skill if you will. Being an extroverted social butterfly meant I am very social most of the time, but I needed to be alone in silence to hear my own thoughts and inner voice. Without solitude, the intuition that guides so much of me would get lost in a swirl of things, people, emotions, and people pleasing. I tried to make situations and relationships that I knew no longer served me work, because I genuinely hated disappointing the people on the other side of the relationships. In some cases, "shape shifting" suited me well. In some, it became my own worst enemy, silencing my inner wisdom, dimming my light and going against what I knew to be true in my heart.

Meanwhile, my ex was the type of person you could talk to easily and wanted to hang out with because he was witty, fun, and broke out into a dance party in your office cubicle just because (that may have happened in real life). He was the type of person that had his friends for a lifetime and actually stayed in contact with them, not just through social media. A genuine connector.

He was not shy to speak to strangers and make new friends; I met one of my best friends to date because he struck up a conversation with her at the pool (not in a creepy way, in a fun "'You should meet my wife, y'all would get along!'" way). I was the yin to his yang, social but not always in party mode. I almost never drank, or didn't drink much, but when I did, I'd only have one drink. We were polar opposites, if you will. His recharge wasn't silence and being home with family, as mine was; his recharge was in doing things constantly and being around a lot of people. Where he felt suffocated by stillness, I found solace. When he often carried the party into our lives, day after day, moon after moon, I found frustration and loneliness. I threw myself deeper and deeper into motherhood, work, and running a household while trying to reconcile how to manage our very different views of what our lives should be, and what they had become.

This was the starting point of finding my voice, and it began to break down the glass walls of our fragile marriage. The truth is, nothing changes unless you change yourself, your situation, or the cast of characters. It's like we were changing clothes in the dressing room, expecting different bodies to appear in the mirror. I had to ask myself, was our situation ever going to get better? It was time I started choosing me!

· · ·

I heard the sound of glass shatter into a thousand pieces as it hit the concrete wall and rained onto the floor, chunks and bits crunching beneath my feet. Suited up in a heavy duty onesie, hair pulled back, and a clear shield covering my face, I felt the anger rising from the soles of my feet as I launched glass bottle after glass bottle against the wall under the dim blue of the room. Rage Against the Machine played in the background, but the sound of my anger and the sound of shattering glass overpowered the music in the room. Every bottle I broke unlocked a deeper and deeper level of hurt, anger and frustration, tears streaming down my face. Five minutes of continuous shattering and I stopped abruptly. Tori pulled me aside, "Were you thinking of your ex as you broke those bottles?"

"Yes," I replied, "Yes, yes, and it felt so good to release all that rage."

Rage. That overwhelming, deep rooted feeling from the soles of your feet, emanating through your whole body. That is what I channeled with every clink of a bottle, every crack of a can. That feeling had to be released and let go, that feeling could not live inside me or it was going to eat me alive. I shattered one last bottle in the rage room and left it all on the floor.

Broken into all these beautiful pieces, the glass was ready to be swept up and recreated much like myself. Jessica Simpson wrote in her memoir, "Whatever you are going through, the sun will come." And it truly did! All the shiny, beautiful, broken pieces of me came back together and I did it all for myself, for my kids, for our best lives. Whatever you are going through, you will find your sparkle again.

· · ·

"You're destroying our marriage!" I shouted. Tears streamed down my face, and it felt like our arguments were always in the same room of the house, the same positioning. He'd be sitting on the navy sofa and I'd be standing on the far side of it, in the middle of the open concept space between our family room and the dining room. That family room wept tears when we fought; I could feel the sad energy as I stood there arguing, defending why I was so blank, so void with him, defending why I had lost that warm and fuzzy feeling, why I shape-shifted into this methodical creature, no longer loveable in his eyes. I had become someone he didn't know or like.

Whenever situations were heightened in our relationship, when the drinking turned up a notch or two, when I wasn't voicing my thoughts or my opinions (until the moment when I did), I felt disregarded. I would argue and fight with him in my head. It was my way of letting out all the things I needed to say but couldn't get out. Then, there were all the things I did say that he overlooked and disregarded as knee-jerk decisions or someone else's thoughts.

"You would never say that," would come his reply. "That sounds like your friend." I was so angry and so hurt inside that on the outside I would shut down. I didn't want to be warm and fuzzy. I didn't want to be anything but heard, seen, accepted, and loved.

I was overwhelmed with life and exhausted from this ongoing rollercoaster. I was not being heard, but when I did speak up and nothing changed. At bedtime I'd lay with our children as they would fall asleep, the soft soundscapes, meditation music and ocean waves crashing upon us. There they would sleep, and I'd weep there next to them as the click of another can opened, or the clank of the glass bottle settled on the tan, brown and black granite in the kitchen. I knew I couldn't hold on much longer and my decision was about to rock all our worlds!

Amidst all my sadness, anger, and frustration, I was running a household, managing children, and working full time. I was throwing myself into work, into busyness, into our children to sustain myself, watching as I became the worst version of myself. But I knew I was still alive, buried deep down inside; I was in there still and I was going to have to dig deep to find her! And I did!

"You can do anything for sixty seconds. Hang on to it, you're almost to the finish line," played through my airpods over and over as Coach Kelly from my FASTER app coached me through sprints, through runs, day after day, after day. "You can do anything!" This mantra played over thirty days became my constant through my divorce. *Lauren you can do anything, hang on to it! You're almost to the finish line! You're going to make it.*

Night after night I'd lay on the extra soft grey carpet in our room, close my eyes and meditate, telling myself I was going to be okay, I was doing it, and not only was I doing it, I was going to do it with love and light. Over and over. Be the love and the light, do right by our kids, post-it's of daily affirmations, podcasts about conscious uncoupling, manifesting courses with my friend Deepika Sandhu: this was my reality, this is and was how I made it through all the hard and harder days. And the days that weren't hard in the beginning were the most beauty filled days. The simple pleasures of silence, time with my kids, making cookies, skateboarding around the neighborhood, running through the back gate to the open park behind our house. Watching our ninety pound, black lab zoom around the yard like a rocket ship was about to get him, while the giant tree branches swayed in the wind. The moments where my children's eyes light up with delight in the simplest of times, and all the world around me feels right—those are the moments I love and live for! The moments I am present and feel alive.

. . •

For so long I questioned myself. Maybe it was because I wasn't enough for him. Maybe if I was sexier, lost more weight, worked out more, loved him more, and didn't have terrible postpartum depression after the birth of our daughter. The harder I pushed him, the more I begged and pleaded for him to stop drinking, the harder he pushed back. I realized, if he wasn't going to change, the change had to come from me—and I had to get off the rollercoaster!

Now, looking back, I realize that you truly cannot make someone do something they don't want to do. No matter how much they love you, or you love them. If they don't want to stop the thing that's hurting them and destroying your relationship, they're not going to do it. No matter how much begging, pleading, crying or ultimatums you give someone. They have to want it more than you want it for them.

Ultimately, the change has to come from yourself. If you speak your mind and see no change in your relationship, if you are not seen and heard, are you okay with that? And if you're not, you have to accept it and make a change for yourself. No one else can do it for you!

You always hear people say, "I stayed for the kids." I didn't want to be one of those people. My parents divorced at a young age. I was four, so growing up in a divorced home with step parents is all I really knew. What I saw from my own parents, even from my grandparents, was this very mature, friendly, and loving relationship, even through divorce. Every holiday my grandparents made a point to have all the family together. I grew up believing divorce could be something beautiful if you let it be. I grew up believing there can be love for one another even after your divorce. You won't always get along or agree, but you can have a decent relationship, and I took all of that to heart when approaching my own divorce. I will say, I now have a new appreciation for my parents, though. They came together with smiles on their faces, all for their love for me and for my benefit. They probably didn't always enjoy being around one another, but they gave me the best possible experience, and they did lead with love.

I believed all through the process of my divorce that this didn't have to be ugly, messy, or angry. Yes... it's filled with hurt and deep rooted sadness, but it could be done in the most loving way and with the most respect for one another as possible, because we owed it to each other and to our children. I was so hurt, I had so much anguish, and all I wanted was for him to pick me, to pick our family over his cravings, but there was nothing I could do or say to make him stop drinking. Despite how badly I felt, I was still determined to do it with as much love, grace, and patience as I could. Even on the really terrible days, when I wanted to hide under my soft white sheets and fuzzy pink blanket, never to come out until months had passed. Like all of us single parents, I still got up and did life with my kids; not just did life, but drenched us in activities and sometimes the simplicity of just being together—in the yard drinking freshly brewed coffee, watching the oversized branches sway in the blue sky. That became life as I knew it, as I wanted it to be. The three of us, simple and sweet. No complications, no mental chatter in my mind, no ugliness, no guilt; we were starting to heal, and I was seeing us all thrive.

· · ·

After years of not listening to myself in my marriage, I found myself in a new relationship, denying the intuition I knew to be true. Again. I knew this new relationship wasn't working for me, and if it wasn't working for me, or if it wasn't the best choice for me, then it couldn't be the best place for my children. Yet I was still there. Still in it.

It started like a scene in a Hollywood rom com. For months, I watched this tall, handsome, dark haired Italian man every day at school drop-off and pickup. And for months I would tell my friend about it. I smiled at him, and he smiled back. I waved at him today. And he smiled back.

On the phone one afternoon at pickup, my girlfriend said to me, "Lauren, You should introduce yourself to him, because if you don't, some other single mom is going to sweep him off the market, now's your chance!"

"But I've never been so bold as to introduce myself to a man. I don't do that. But you're right! I'm going to do it!"

It was a Friday afternoon pickup, and I timed it just right. His car was parked across the street from mine, and as he walked across, I stepped out of my car and headed for the sidewalk just as he did. "Hi, I'm Lauren, I see you every day at pick up and thought I'd introduce myself." The handsome Italian greeted me with a smile, extended his hand out and introduced himself. In that moment I felt a connection that sparked my soul. The moment he shook my hand, it was as if every fiber of my being came alive, and I could feel myself glowing from within and radiating outward. It was magic!

Why was I trying to make this relationship work for me...

Why? Love. That's why.

In my heart I deeply loved my handsome Italian, and felt connected to him in a way I have never been connected before. He made me feel loved, safe and secure in his arms and in his presence. When the world felt hard he would wrap me up, and the world would fade away. I was safe and could relinquish control.

But over time deep down, in the depths of my heart, although I desperately wanted to ignore it, I felt like the confines of our relationship continued to grow greater and greater. He once said to me in conversation, "Why would you throw away love, when love is so hard to find in this world?" Love is hard to find and I never looked at it as throwing "us" away. I looked at our relationship with so many wonderful memories, with so much love. In some ways, my handsome Italian brought me back to life from the ashes. He made me see that love and deep connection with another was still possible. That someone will love me in all my needy, messy moments of life; at least that's how I felt to start. And then as I started to feel more and more confined by the differences in our children, in our parenting styles, and in our daily lives, I began to feel depleted, like I had nothing left to give.

The worst love to throw away is the love you have for yourself. That hurts the most... and I could feel myself being consumed up by our life together, getting lost in trying to rush about to make our schedules work. I knew it was time for me to step away before I was swallowed whole. One of the hardest things for me to do was acknowledge and accept the signs from the Universe, then set that greater plan into motion to release what is no longer serving me. The amount of time, effort, and stress that ending these relationships has caused me...if you have ever known me, you will know that I am not a half-in kind of person. I am an all-in or all-out type of person—there is no in between. And once we hit the in-between point, we have a situation! Like a real situation! Because in that moment what appeared to be a "knee-jerk reaction" or "short-sighted" was actually a woman who had contemplated all the thoughts accumulated in her head for so long that they have now all come to a head, and needed to be addressed with rapid speed.

Old patterns and habits die hard—even when you can see them and the Universe is shouting at you saying, "This isn't right! You need to make a change!" It's hard to acknowledge, it's hard to break the habit. It's even harder when it comes to matters of the heart. Since the start of writing this chapter, my tall, handsome Italian man and I had stopped talking for a long period of time. I could feel myself shrinking into a tiny box again, losing myself, and I knew I needed to be true to my inner wisdom. It broke my heart to break his. I never wanted to be that person in our relationship. And as painful as it was for me, and as heartbroken as I felt, I knew it was the right choice. I needed to be alone, to come back to myself, to come back into my own body and mind and he respected that. For months we fell silent, like complete strangers passing in the street.

All the reasons made it that much harder for me to take pause from my handsome Italian, to be away from him for months. It wasn't that he was a bad guy, he was a great guy! He's a great guy for me! Unfortunately, blending a family is just not for what my little family of three needed. And my kids always come first!

Our relationship felt seamless to start, almost organic. We both had children about the same age, he had two boys and I had a boy and a girl, and they all went to school together.

It felt like we all belonged together, and that's what I wanted to continue to believe in my heart as time passed.

Our children had love/hate relationships with one another, perhaps very sibling-like in some ways. My siblings are twenty-six years my junior, so the idea of "growing up" with siblings doesn't resonate with me in the least. I didn't expect them to get along all the time, but I also didn't expect to feel as though the confines of our relationship were being boxed in smaller and smaller because of differences in our children. Our relationship started to feel diminished by invisible walls and internally suffocated me with anxiety. The kind of anxiety that you can feel deep in your belly, crawling up your chest getting tighter and tighter, your heart pounding and you can't breathe—that kind of anxiety. The kind that makes you want to run out of the room or leave the very place you are and never look back.

The Universe works in mysterious ways, guiding you and showing you literally before your eyes; it's like the sleight of hand at the poker table, or an optical illusion you know isn't right but you want to believe. Finding your voice, listening to yourself, your instincts isn't just a one-time lesson—it's a life lesson that repeats and manifests in so many ways in your life. The key was not just acknowledging it, it was to hear what lies deep within, and then choosing to take action. I knew it, I had seen it, the Universe was showing me, yet I was continuously denying it. I had to un-become who I had been in my marriage, I had to release myself from the tiny boxes I had shape-shifted myself into—silent, passive, frustrated, lonely—to stand up for myself.

I am continuing to find my voice, continuing to learn to lean into that inner wisdom. Recognizing my patterns, learning to step into my truth, vocalizing my wants and needs. Showing up for myself, more than ever, but from a different place—a place of more self-compassion and grace. These lessons continue and carry on over and over. The lesson and reminder to choose YOU, to bet on yourself, to choose yourself! Because you're worth it!

"You only get this one life," one of my dearest friends always says, "In this one life, you can do hard things."

It's hard to choose yourself when you love someone so much, when you're an eternal optimist, a recovering people pleaser; when you want to believe that circumstances or people are going to and will change for the better. But not choosing me was eating me alive. Wondering yet again if I could hold on—if I could make it work. I loved him after all, shouldn't that be enough when we had the connection we had.

When I told my kids we stopped talking, they didn't say much. Kids are funny that way; they absorb your own energy and mirror it back to you. As a mom, I try to share lessons I learned in my own life along the way in hopes that one day they look back, having learned from how my relationship unfolded between the handsome Italian and I; that you can love someone very deeply, but know when to walk away, to choose yourself, to tend to your own heart and soul and trust your intuition. But also, to recognize when you're too frightened to let your guard down. I hope that I taught my children that when you let down your guard for the right person, who meets you where you need to be met, allows you to speak your truth unapologetically, and loves you unconditionally, that there is beauty in the mess. All of those moments, the good, the bad, and the uncertain, can all lead to joy.

My next chapter was where I became so clear in manifesting what I needed and wanted, where I was so aligned with myself and the Universe. Where I tended to my heart and the needs of my children more than ever before. Where I unapologetically communicated what I truly needed and went after what I wanted. Where I realized relationships don't have to be a one-size fits all box and that love does exist and you can be real, raw, messy, and still be loveable and wanted. The chapter where I found my voice, to speak my truth to him, to break the confines of the box I was stuck in.

The chapter where I stopped limiting my beliefs about who I am, what things should look like, or how they should be. Where I was fully present for my children and for myself. Where I sat in silence and it was glorious and not deafening or defeating as it once felt when I first left my marriage.

While the days are long but the years are short, I do my best to soak in the time I have with my children. When I was newly divorced, it was agonizing to not have my kids in my presence all the time, knowing that it was my own doing, that I made this choice consciously. But once I learned to reframe the negative into a positive, they are now getting the best, strongest, most confident and happy version of me, and the healthiest version of their father. My heart could finally be at peace, and I am the most aligned I've felt in a long time.

Before Elizabeth handed over the keys to the new buyer after the sale of her house, she hugged me tight and told me it was all going to be okay. I sat on the hardwood floor of the empty family room alone, where I had once laid sobbing about my life in ruins, this time tears streaking my cheeks in happiness as I looked back at a chapter truly coming to a close. She was right, it all was and is okay! My life is better than okay, and I did it! It wasn't always graceful or perfect, but along the way I've learned to give myself grace, trust my intuition and follow the compass of my heart—it will always guide you back to your true self.

Lauren is a proud mom of two and can most often be found on the sidelines—cheering loud and proud at her kids' sports games (yes, she's *that* mom). A spiritual gangster with a heart full of optimism, she's equal parts Barre babe and Pilates princess, always chasing good vibes and better posture.

She calls the Dallas-Fort Worth area home, where her days are filled with carpool lines, coffee runs, and moments of deep gratitude. Fiercely devoted to her children and passionate about personal growth, Lauren believes in showing up, speaking truth, and loving big.

This is her first published work—a labor of love born from her own healing journey. She hopes her story helps other women feel seen, supported, and a little less alone. More to come—she's just getting started.

6

THE DOOR I CHOSE

By Kathryn Bisland

This is bizarre.

Those words kept running through my mind as I scrolled through pages of random men's profiles on a sperm selling website.

Hair color, height, nationality, hobbies, interests, how many families his sperm has already been sold to (meaning how many half siblings my future child would have?).

How bizarre (sang the band OMC in my mind on repeat).

No Canadians though because, fun fact, in Canada sperm donation is unpaid. So not much interest as a result. My selection was a long list of American and European men.

I stopped scrolling momentarily as my eyes lingered on a gorgeous young Scottish man with piercing eyes, and curly dark brown hair (kind of looked like my dad, of course he did). Ahhh, good at sports and he plays the guitar? Perfection!

You know the saying when you meet your person, "when you know, you know"? Well, it's the same for picking out the sperm donor for your future child. This was the guy, or should I say, the sperm for me.

Right, sperm chosen. Now what's left? I thought to myself.

I whipped out my handy intrauterine insemination checklist from my doctor to see where I was at in the process:

Cycle monitoring: bloodwork and a daily internal pelvic exam to check out my growing ovaries in real-time? Every morning at 7 a.m. from day one of my cycle until ovulation, which was around day sixteen back then (extra long for me, hurray!), and everything is in perfect working order—check!

Egg reserve blood test: To check how my geriatric (what you called a woman looking to conceive at age thirty-eight or above back in 2017, they've since become much more politically correct and now refer to us as "advanced maternal age," so sweet of them to take the sting out of it!) eggs were holding up. Hurray, eggs at moderate level—check! I'm like a spry thirty-four to thirty-six years old instead of a thirty-eight years old, gnarly past her pregnancy-prime old lady.

Meeting with the fertility doctor: I got my results from the above information, and a meeting where he skipped into the room and gleefully announced he could get me pregnant no problem—in fact, he could have me knocked up by June—check!

Visiting the therapist to assess and then bestow her certification that I am of sane mind to be granted the privilege of going through with the IUI process, even though we discussed that I was still in an emotionally abusive marriage with a functioning alcoholic and pothead who was not supportive of me becoming a mother and had no intention of making it easy for me to do this (talk about a dream home for a child to grow up in right?), given the all clear—check!

And now, the final step in the process: choose a sperm donor and buy it.

Hmmmm...

My finger lingered over the "add to cart" button.

But I heard a quiet voice inside my head saying, just wait a bit to do this.

And so, I closed the page after starring my perfect Scottish sperm dude for future ease of purchasing, and quickly shut my laptop as I heard the front door to my condo open. I absolutely did not want to be caught doing what I was doing.

The abusive husband mentioned above had just walked in.

I never knew my life would be like this.

Well, not consciously anyway.

Being a child in the eighties was a bizarre time to grow up in. Labeled the slacker generation, us Gen X kids were screwed right from the start.

Imagine receiving the message that you were a slacker (a.k.a. having no willpower or follow through, so destined to be unsuccessful) before you even had a chance.

I'm not sure if it was our baby boomer parents fearing losing control over us or a bigger matrix conspiracy, but that societal messaging was impossible to ignore and it ensured that regardless of your childhood, you would never amount to anything because you didn't even have it in you to try. Brutal right?

Combine that with my less than idyllic childhood—walking on eggshells because of my functioning alcoholic father (who was charming in public but angry and irritable in private), whose main target was my mom and whom I was positioned to be the protector of.

Super tense and super inappropriate by today's standards, making me, the child, take on adult responsibilities.

I was the "good," "easy" and "mature" child whom they never had to worry about—we now know that simply meant I learned early on that my needs didn't matter, and if I wanted to be safe, I better be hypervigilant about the adults around me, lest the dense unwavering tension fog lift momentarily and morph into a big old brawl.

My dad's favorite things to say to me on repeat in his thick Scottish accent were, "Get oot of my road," (Get out of my way, because I, simply by being, am always in the way).

Or, "Don't annoy me," (I'm annoying).

My mom tried to help by telling me early on that my dad had a "drinking problem," and then tried to explain what that meant to a child.

God bless her, but all I heard was, "Your dad is only capable of loving you so much, so take what you can get." That eventually morphed into the limiting belief that not even my own dad could love me fully, thus something must be wrong with me.

This translated further into, "I am unlovable and unworthy and can be abandoned at any time because love is conditional on me fixing everything and not being a burden by being myself."

Damn, that's some shit—my past therapists would be so proud of my awareness!

Then add in childhood bullying, as I grew up in a neighborhood where I was the minority as a white girl, which they called reverse racism back then, where (if you can believe it) I was picked on and belittled for being white. Bizarre right?

No matter what I did, I just couldn't fit it with my peers (Human Design would have been really helpful back then—I'm a manifestor, which means I naturally repel people for protection).

So, the quest to make myself small, people please, and give away all of my power became a baseline for my existence. All so I would be safe at home and in the wild world outside.

Clearly through my subconscious limiting beliefs and programming from childhood, there was no chance in hell it was going to end up any other way than this.

But I also grew up watching *Cinderella* in the eighties, so I was convinced that it didn't matter how many people I let treat me like shit along the way, if I sat demurely and bided my time, then my eventual rescue by the prince was inevitable.

Unfortunately, I also must have read "The Frog Prince" too, so kissing a ton of frogs also seemed like the smart thing to do.

Being immersed in disempowering female storylines (my favorite movie was *Pretty Woman*—try explaining and defending *that* story line to gen Z females now!) where I was powerless and life happened to me because it was out of my control throughout my youth, led me to continually fantasize about a man saving me from my horrible life.

So, when I was in my early 20s working at a bar booth in a weekend trade show and locked eyes with a man who seemed to see into the depths of my soul—and then ran into him again exactly one year later at the same event—damn, I was hooked on the narrative of "this is fate."

He was tall and lanky, with a heavy brow and piercing blue eyes that seemed to exist on a face with a perpetual, slight scowl, and shaggy dark blond hair.

He had an edgy rock and roll vibe, think late nineties grunge, slightly unhealthy but yet alluring. Turns out he had been the front man for a semi-successful Canadian band back in the day, playing shows with future Canadian megastars like Sloan and Finger Eleven—if you're up on your Canadian nineties alternative music stars.

When he looked at me, he made me feel like all he saw was me; his energy enveloped and consumed me, his eyes never leaving mine and his slightly amused smile confirming I was presenting myself favorably to him.

He made me feel seen and chosen for the first time in my life.

I was twenty-four turning twenty-five, and he was ten years my senior. The allure of my power to captivate an experienced older man and the allure of his ability to capture and control a damaged younger girl ignited an intense trauma bond that would trap us for over a decade.

This is such a key moment to emphasize.

When we encounter someone at a soul level and both souls have had their fair share of difficulties and pain through life—that they *haven't* healed from yet—we often bond in these moments. Especially when we feel comfort in the similarity of the other person's story—"no one understands me like they do"—so we call it true love, soulmate level stuff.

But is it?

If the version of me now were to meet this version of him back then, I would have still noticed him, because I would have energetically recognized his pain as something similar to the pain within me.

But beyond that, I wouldn't have given him a second glance.

The rock and roll vibe? I would have seen through it to what it meant lay just beneath the surface: addiction struggles.

The perpetual scowl? I would have immediately translated that to mean deep seated anger and resentment—that was not my responsibility to fix.

The intense and penetrating stare? Obviously scanning me to evaluate the level of my daddy issues, a.k.a. my controllability.

The slightly amused smile? Clearly his feelings of superiority over me as he watched me perform for him and try to please him.

But back then, I was filtering my experience of him through a different lens, one that was highly wounded and primed for an expert in manipulation and control to come and "sweep me off my feet."

In my early twenties I had lost touch with the ability to think for myself, because I learned the hard way that doing that was dangerous for my overall safety.

Thus, when two traumatized and unhealed people like us met and connected, we now know it was a trauma bond that locked us together.

We were destined to recreate that trauma with each other on an unconscious level over and over again because it was all that we knew of love and relationships.

It was familiar, it was where we unconsciously felt safe—even though it hurt.

That is not love.

But back then we didn't have that level of awareness or understanding.

So at that moment, twenty-two years ago, I believed to the depths of my soul, that I had fallen madly, deeply, and rapturously in love with my soulmate.

Something he confirmed as true for him too. Apparently, a psychic once told him that his one true love would be considerably younger than him (he got me with that hook, line, and sinker).

Boom! "It's fate!" my mind screamed at me.

Finally, here was my prince. I was being rescued from my shitty life.

Boy did he "rescue" me in the beginning. Well, more like he love-bombed me.

He would take me to amazing dinners at downtown restaurants I had only heard about in magazines.

We had late night calls (drunken calls—red flag anyone?), and he would leave long and elaborate voicemails telling me I was the only one who understood him.

We had homemade dinners at his downtown apartment where he sang to me, and we danced in the kitchen while he laughed at all my jokes and told me I was a woman (not a girl like most guys my age referred to me, but a real woman!).

He would randomly take me shopping for dresses or shoes at fancy downtown boutiques, then whisk me to cool events to meet all his "sophisticated" friends who knew all the cool bars and DJs (hell, some of his friends were even DJs!).

I would wear my beautiful, elegant new dresses and shoes, and I would feel like a real woman instead of some stupid white trash girl from Scarborough.

Experiencing these moments triggered a sneaking suspicion that I had somehow finally risen above the disappointments of my youth, because here I was hanging out with older people in exclusive clubs, bypassing the lines, and being made to feel important.

And in the early days, he was forever professing to be madly and deeply in love with me—constantly and consistently.

I felt seen, I felt worthy, I felt vindicated, I felt alive.

Until I didn't.

It started out subtle, like it always does.

A few more days between the phone calls from him, leaving me feeling anxious and needy—but he did still call, I reasoned.

Him canceling plans last minute with vague reasons as to why, giving me a sense of him not being into me and activating my innate desperateness to figure out what I was doing wrong—but he still kept some plans with me, I reminded myself.

Sharp one-liner criticisms about me being young and dumb sandwiched between praise for my emotional maturity, so I didn't quite notice but developed a growing sense of insecurity. It still confirmed the main storyline that I was a woman not a girl though, I determined in my mind.

While this bread crumbing may be obvious to a younger generation reading my story, it's important to understand that all Gen Xers (born approximately 1965–1982) and many early millennials (born starting in the mid-eighties) didn't have this language or these tools—so it was challenging to see at the time.

The baby boomers who were our parents might have started a revolution in the sixties, but they sure passed on a ton of generational trauma, like burying one's head in the sand—which I did to perfection, let me tell you!

My favorite mantra to excuse his behavior was, "He doesn't treat me as badly as my dad treats my mom."

Please note: This is a very low benchmark. My dad treated my mom like crap (and my mom allowed my dad to treat her like crap).

I watched my dad blame my mom for the disappointments in his life, and use her as an outlet to express his dissatisfaction and frustration because he had left Scotland and came to Canada for a better life—yet he was still trapped.

I watched my mom accept it and be the victim, allowing herself to be dumped on because she didn't have the tools to stand up for herself. I wondered why no one in her family was helping us get out of this situation. Surely, they could see that it wasn't good.

I learned very quickly that if there was a problem, it was never your fault. You either blamed someone else, or you were the victim of circumstance—and no one was going to help you.

I was shown a love that was judged, that criticized, that was conditional—based on how good you made the other person look and feel.

I was modeled on a love that could and would be withheld if you were unable to anticipate others' needs, fix their problems, and keep them happy.

I learned that my purpose and worth were wrapped up in what I achieved—because when I achieved, or looked beautiful, or made others laugh because I was so witty, well-spoken, and intelligent, I made them look good. And so, it was okay for me to stick around.

But if I didn't do that, then I was a burden—an annoyance, something they didn't really want to have to deal with. My dad showed this through ignoring me, and my mom through escaping into TV rather than playing or engaging with me.

I was fearful in love because the threat of being rejected and abandoned always loomed large for me.

So my mantra of "He doesn't treat me as badly as my dad treats my mom" was my touchstone to prove that I wasn't recreating my childhood trauma. How could I be, if this love was better than that love?

But everything is relative to what it's being compared against. And I didn't have much to compare it to.

So it was what I told myself to lie about the situation I had found myself in.

And as a result, as his mistreatment of me grew, I never registered it—because, hey, it wasn't as bad as my dad was to my mom. Win!

I also told myself regularly, "I have never experienced a love as intense and fulfilling as this before—it's better than anything I've ever had."

But keep in mind I had a history of kissing a lot of frogs. (And to be frank, anyone who was a healthy man came across to me as intensely boring and unattractive—thanks to my innate sense for chaos in my life due to my childhood.)

So this mantra allowed me to keep comparing him to the losers I had dated in high school and early university, to which he always fared better. Win!

And finally, I was driven by a fear of being alone. Somehow I had developed a belief along the way that being in a relationship (no matter how crappy) was success.

And so, by being in this partnership, I was a success. Huge win!

When he proposed (by showing me a ring and saying, "So are you gonna marry me or what?") I was twenty-eight, fully immersed in our trauma bond cycle of "the calm before the storm," "the huge fight," and "the passionate make-up"—which happened on a monthly basis back then.

Aaaand remember—I viewed being married by thirty to someone who wasn't as bad as my dad, and much better than anyone else I'd ever dated, as a big "success." Thus, it was a no-brainer to say yes.

It was a no-brainer to the people in my life at the time to fully support this as well—except for one friend who told me it was a bad idea. But don't worry, I quickly ended that friendship. She was obviously jealous of my "success." Who needs friends like that?

So we got married. And everything was perfect.

For him.

Because now he had me right where he wanted me.

I woke up on the morning of March 17, 2016, with a pit in my stomach and a "what the fuck just happened" feeling racing through my body.

You see, it was the morning of my thirty-seventh birthday, and while I sluggishly made my way to the kitchen to brew some coffee, I was struggling to comprehend how that could actually be possible.

I stared at the percolating coffee, and as each drip fell into the brew, I realized that was how quickly the last six years of my life had sped by.

In an instant—like a drip of coffee falling from the machine into the pot.

WTF?

The last age I remembered being was thirty-one, yet according to all external visuals, reality was telling me I was thirty-seven.

But this wasn't where I imagined I would be at thirty-seven. It was far from it. How did that happen?

I felt numb, dull, disconnected.

And then I felt dread.

The time to bury my head in the sand was up, and the realization that it was time to face the truth loomed in front of me like an ominous dark shadow.

For my thirty-seventh birthday, I was gifted with two doors. I was at my proverbial fork in the road, and what I would decide here would seal my fate forever—either chaining me to misery or dropping me out of a plane in the sky with no guarantee of a parachute to save me.

When I express it like that, it seems an easy choice—jump, you say, jump out of the fucking plane!

But when you are immersed in the actual reality of what you have known versus the unknown, the familiar chaos always becomes the loudest voice.

Because in its familiarity, it promises safety and comfort. It is what you know. And we are hard-wired as humans to always revert back to what we know when we are unaware that we have the power to choose.

"Good thing we're not having kids. You'd be such a terrible mom anyway—look at you, you can't even get out of bed early in the morning. You'd never be able to handle kids."

"Only sheeple who are unenlightened have kids. It's the ultimate method of control by the system and government. Only stupid people have kids because they are being manipulated into being controlled."

"You know there is absolutely no difference between you drinking coffee in the morning and me drinking or smoking pot—you're just as addicted as I am. In fact, yours is worse because coffee has the exact same effect on your body as cocaine. You'd never be able to give it up for a kid."

Things like this had been said to me daily for the last six years, since the moment my ex went in for a check-up and came back dropping a bomb on me as he entered the house (before even saying hello): "Well, it looks like I'm shooting blanks, and that's fine. I never wanted kids anyway."

That was a huge lie. Before we got married, we had discussed kids—he even told me he was certain he was going to have twin boys (twins run in my family; my grandpa was a twin) and he even had the names picked out: Hollis and Silas. (FYI, I never officially agreed to those names).

If he had said he didn't want to be a father, that would have been a deal breaker for me (yes, yes, ironic—that's the deal breaker, not the addiction and abuse...) because I always knew I desired to be a mother.

So, on the morning of my thirty-seventh birthday, when it dawned on me that I had no idea where the last six years of my life had gone, shortly thereafter—once I had consumed my morning cup of coffee (aka my apparent cocaine fix)—I realized I couldn't remember the last six years of my life because I had been living through trauma and emotional abuse.

To ignore it, I had become a workaholic, distracting myself from the isolation and loneliness I had been experiencing. I immersed myself in superficial problems in the workplace, solving them at rapid speed to feel a sense of purpose and worth, because at home I felt worthless, weak, and incompetent.

After all, my dream of being a mom was apparently now out of my control, as per my ex's medical diagnosis and decree that we would NOT be exploring any alternative methods.

And this was fully reinforced with daily reminders about how terrible I would be at it and that only fools did it, so why even bother?

When I was thirty-one, it was easy to say to myself, "Oh, I'm only thirty-one. I have plenty of time. I don't want to be a mom until I'm thirty-three, anyway."

Then I turned thirty-three, but it was still easy to brush away the nagging feeling that something was missing by saying to myself, "Oh, I'm only thirty-three. I actually don't want to be a mom until I'm thirty-five, anyway."

And even at thirty-five, I still said, "Oh, I have plenty of time, I don't really want to be a mom just yet."

But on the morning of my thirty-seventh birthday, I could no longer run and hide. As a child and teen of the eighties/nineties, the societal message drilled into me was that once you neared forty getting pregnant would be impossible (which actually now has been debunked, science has found that on average there is an 82 percent chance that a woman 35-39 can conceive within a year if they are having sex 1-2 times per week—so let's stop that generational trauma myth right here, right now).

And as I looked around my condo in downtown Toronto, seeing the giant ziploc bag of pot under my coffee table, half empty packs of cigarettes and tiny leftover roaches on my coffee table, and the four clear garbage bags filled to the brim with empty tall boy beer cans that obstructed my view of the beautiful city on my balcony—I couldn't lie to myself anymore.

I had missed the last six years of my life because I had been hiding in plain view.

Being what my ex had expected me to be as per his "fuck the system" Gen X rock and roll lifestyle persona.

Acquiescing to his authority out of fear that his rage would eventually turn on me (which of course it did, quite regularly now).

Weary from attempting to communicate my concerns to him, only to be gaslit and have everything turned back onto me so fast that it made me feel crazy, and like I couldn't trust my own thoughts.

He had told me to give up on my dream of being a mother, for him and "for us," but as I looked around that morning with clear eyes for the first time in six years, I could see that who he had become was not his true potential that I had focused on when we first met.

His true potential was buried in his disappointment in life, in his unmet needs, in his personal trauma, in the demons that he battled daily and was losing ground to. His alcoholism and his chosen methods of escapism now controlled his identity—and had taken over my life too (because I had let it).

He expected me to give up my dream of being a mother, but he had no intention of giving up his addictions in return. In an effort to fully control me, he had demanded that I relinquish motherhood, which I had slowly been loosening my grip on without realizing over the last six years. But in return, all I was getting was a shell of a man.

One who drank and got drunk daily.

"Please get help for your drinking," I said, "I'm drowning under the weight of your alcoholism."

"No," he said, "I don't need any help, I can stop at any time."

"So please stop."

"No," he said, "but I'll drink less." Which of course he didn't do.

My "dream" life, the one he wanted me to give up having a baby for, consisted of living with:

A man who would wake me up every morning by hacking up copious amounts of phlegm due to a voracious appetite for consuming weed and cigarettes daily, then act like it was normal even though it clearly wasn't. He was ten years older than me. Did he have cancer (like many of my family members)? Did he have a chronic disease (like my mother)? Was he going to get sick and die and then leave me? My abandonment issues were massively triggered by this.

A man whose shift at the restaurant finished at midnight, but who wouldn't come home until 3-4 a.m. I would lay awake night after night waiting for him with a pit in my stomach, often texting him but receiving no response. I had read the classic book *He's Just Not That into You*, so deep down I knew this meant he didn't really want to be with me because if he did then he would. And he wasn't, so clearly I was to blame because I wasn't enough.

A man who told me he had lost all interest in sex with me because I was so "vanilla in bed." Again, blaming me, making me feel less than so I would get wrapped up in my own insecurities instead of realizing that when a previously highly sexual man loses interest in you, it's usually because he's getting it from somewhere else.

A man who would fly off in a rage at me at the drop of the hat, which I could always tell was coming due to a particular look in his eye—just like my dad did with my mom. Sometimes for something as simple as not scooping the cat's litter exactly when he thought it should be done and then being berated for it (used as another example of how I would be a terrible mother).

Or for something more serious, like me asking him not to drink so much at the airport before a flight home, leading to him hurling loudly whispered abuse at me (that others could hear) the entire plane ride home, and being ditched at the airport without a key at 11 p.m. at night—twice.

This was what he wanted me to give up my dream of being a mother for, this life.

A life that was slowly choking me under its weight.

It was not a fair exchange.

Here I was in a drug and alcohol-fueled world, yet I was pretty straight-laced. Hell, a glass of wine gave me a buzz, and two made me drunk. I didn't smoke cigarettes or pot, and I never touched hard drugs. Yet I was surrounded by others' addictions. *What the fuck?*

I was so done with carrying the burdens of other people's destructive behavior.

Doing so had me beaten down and depressed. My pain was palpable from years of presenting to the world that all was well and I was wonderful.

And I wasn't going to fucking take it anymore.

I used to go for long walks—sometimes twice a day—in the east side of downtown Toronto. One day, shortly after my birthday, something made me stop outside of a beautiful church at the corner of Church and Adelaide Street. I walked in and went straight to the table of candles—the ones you light for souls who have passed. I put in my dollar donation, lit a candle, and walked over to the pew. I began to pray.

"My baby," I whispered in the shadows of the church's arches, "I am ready for you. I call you to come to me."

Tears streamed down my face as I pleaded to a soul I couldn't see but felt with all of my being.

"I don't know how, but I am ready for you. Please come to me. I love you."

I did that every day for two weeks.

And then I went to the fertility clinic.

I told my ex I was doing it. To which he said, "Go ahead, but I don't support you."

After watching me actually go through with it, he became more drastic with his threats, "I will not help raise this child at all if you do this."

And I didn't care. I didn't want his help. He was crazy if he thought I would let him treat this child the way he treated me. The minute he told me he wasn't going to get any help to overcome his addictions, I shut off from him and the relationship.

I was now in lone wolf mode.

As he lay there, passed out snoring in the bedroom, I would rage-cry as I listened to Fiona Apple on my earbuds, whisper-screaming my anger at him through the door, tears streaming down my face.

When I was alone in the condo, I would sit on the bed and plead with the universe, begging for my freedom.

"I just want to be free!" I would scream over and over again, the cityscape of downtown Toronto blurry through eyes full of tears.

One day after a cycle monitoring appointment at the fertility clinic, I almost collapsed as I sat on the curb behind the building, unable to walk one more step. I was so overcome with grief by the people whom I had just shared space with—people with real fertility issues, who were dealing with the inability to naturally conceive and carry their babies, and this was their last hope.

The guilt I felt was almost too much to bear, because I had been given a clean bill of health—remember the gleeful, "I can have you pregnant by June!" fertility doctor? I was there not because I had any issue getting pregnant, but because of the person I was choosing to be in a relationship with.

As I sat there crying on the curb, there was no way to avoid the question:

Why was I in a relationship with him?

When he saw that I was going to go through with it, I recall him saying, "Well, maybe one day when the kid is older, I'll actually learn to love the little fucker."

There was no way in hell I was going to let him near my baby.

So maybe that's why I hesitated that afternoon as the mouse arrow hovered over the "add to cart" button on the sperm website.

We often get these feelings of "not yet"—whispers from our intuition.

In this case, it was the whisper of my unborn baby. She had a plan and had already picked out her dad—and it wasn't this young Scottish sperm donor or my ex.

And because I had opened the conversation with her via my prayers in the church, she had become (without my consciously realizing it at the time) my beautiful guardian angel—guiding me with silent but knowing nudges and inclinations toward the right next step. Including holding off on buying the sperm.

I have always said that Scarlett saved my life. Our soul connection was so strong that even when I tried my damndest not to listen, I still heard her calling me. Her voice in my heart and in my mind was the catalyst to break the generational trauma of abuse and addiction I had been enmeshed in—and had successfully recreated in my adult life.

I may, at the time, have placed a zero value on myself, but I held her potential in the highest esteem and refused to subject her to the pain I had endured.

And so she became my purpose—my reason to change everything in my life so she could join me earth side.

And the idea of her rekindled my love affair with myself.

She connected me to a strength inside of me that had always been there, but had become a soft whisper. Now, because of her, it was a ferocious roar that was impossible to—nor did I want to—ignore.

And nothing was going to stop me from holding her in my arms—or remembering to respect myself again as I carried out my mission.

When my ex and I finally separated after one last public blow-up (at the twenty-year high school reunion I had just spent the last eleven months planning), I knew it was finally over.

When people asked me that night where my husband went, I looked them straight in the eye and said, "He left. Our marriage is over."

And when I finally saw him three days later, he said, "Let's talk about how we can move on from this—you'll just never speak of the reunion ever again," I responded with, "No. We are going to talk about how this marriage is over." I looked at him, and I saw in his eyes the recognition that I was truly serious—and it was over.

The game had ended after twelve years, and there was nothing left for him to take, because I had walked through the door to my new life—and he was not welcome there. We had officially gotten onto two separate trains. He knew it. And he didn't fight it.

At some point after that, he said to me, "You know, you're unlike any other woman I have ever dated before. I just can't figure you out."

That always stuck with me, because whether he realized it or not, what he meant when he said he couldn't figure me out was that he couldn't break me.

That was very powerful for me.

No matter what he—or life—has thrown at me, it has never broken me. I am still standing.

And this morning, almost seven years after the fact, I'm acutely aware that here I am—actually holding this precious, beautiful soul in my arms and experiencing the power of our bond as she snuggles in closer, contentedly whispering "Mommy" with closed eyes and a soft smile on her face.

I am now living a life I once only dreamed of.

When I realized in the aftermath that I was still standing, what did I do with that awareness?

I remembered that the soul who was still standing was who I really was.

And I fell madly in love with her.

Because she is powerful. She is courageous. She is persistent. And she has never given up, no matter how tough it has gotten.

She is me.

And more importantly—she is you.

Kathryn is an emerging writer & speaker, having done freelance articles for online lifestyle magazines, being a part of this incredible book, and most recently speaking live to a room of over 100 dance educators at a live seminar at the Toronto Dance Teacher Expo 2025. She has cultivated her past dance training & experiences, and is now an online entrepreneur. She is the co-founder of JazzTapClass.com, a done-for-you jazz and tap syllabus designed to help teachers deliver real results to their once-a-week recreational dancers. She leads the Skool Community: Dance Teacher providing resources to parents and teachers of the once-a-week rec dancers at all levels. She also stars in Dance With Miss Kathryn, her YouTube channel that brings the magic to kids ages 2–7 with playful, free ballet, jazz, and tap classes built on the same technique-first foundation.

But her most important role is being the proud mama of two gorgeous little souls, and being in a healthy relationship with her partner, who shares her passion of getting curious about their triggers, and breaking generational trauma together one day at a time, both for themselves and for their two littles. Kathryn is most aligned when the four of them are all singing, dancing and laughing together while listening to eighties new wave music in their kitchen. You can find her on Instagram (@kathrynbisland, @dancewithmisskathryn, @jazztapclass), Tiktok (@subconscious_success) and YouTube (@dancewithmisskathryn).

NATHALIE **PERRON**

To my children, my partner, my sisters, my mother, and my friends—your encouragement and unwavering love have carried me through the writing of this chapter and so many of my life's endeavors. You are my roots and my wings.

To the father of my children—thank you for showing me what true love feels like. Though life guided us along different paths so we could grow and expand in our own ways, I will always be proud of the journey we shared and who we have become.

To Deepika Sandhu, creator of Soul Sparks Press, and to the gifted Fareeha—your leadership and guidance have been a light on this path.

To all the courageous authors of this book—thank you for daring to share your stories and for allowing your light to shine so others may find their way.

To Renée Hartleib and Anne Bérubé—your mentorship, encouragement, and guidance made it possible for this chapter to find its voice.

And to you, dear reader—thank you for opening your heart to my story. My hope is that within these pages you find a spark of courage, a whisper of possibility, and a reminder that hope is always within reach, even in life's most unexpected chapters.

With love, Nathalie

. . .

AUDREY **ALICE**

SIMON - Thank you for the good times, for the lessons, and for our beautiful boys. Thank you for continuing to protect them, and me, from beyond. I hope you're blasting some Tom Petty up there and having a party every day.

ALICE - Thank you for your unconditional love, for staying connected across oceans and timezones and for opening the way for me.

JULIE - Thank you for listening to the same stories until I was able to put them to rest, for seeing my strengths when I forgot them and for always getting me back on the high-flying disc!

LAURA - Thank you for loving all my weirdness, for sharing yours with me and for celebrating all the wins, no matter how small.

HUGO, OSCAR & ARTHUR - Thank you for finding me in this lifetime, for choosing me as your Maman, for trusting in me and for choosing love over everything else, always. You will forever be my greatest accomplishment. Thank you for keeping me going when I didn't know how, just by being yourselves. I love you forever and eternity—for all of our past and future lives.

· · •

MICHELLE WINCELL
O'LEARY

I express my heartfelt gratitude for the abundance of consciousness available in each present moment. The brilliance of conscious awareness, as the gentle unfolding of one's being becomes transformed, offers exponential expansion and growth. I am continuously becoming more in every breath, engaged with conscious evolution for all.

I am infinitely grateful for Jim Self, Roxane Burnett, and the Mastering Alchemy community, as their wisdom has illuminated my path. Jim teaches that, while finding these higher states of being may seem simple, it's not always easy. Together, we navigate the vast sea of collective consciousness, filled with love and mastery.

I appreciate my Dream Team, fellow alchemists, and the many wise mirrors who encourage me to shine my light and share my joy. I learn from and with you, and feel your love. We journey together, co-creating a space of happiness and wellbeing for everyone.

To the spark of light that is Deepika Sandhu, thank you for encouraging me to tell my story and share my wisdom. Your belief in me ignited my energy. I learned more than I imagined I would through the process of expressing and sharing this personal expression of my story.

This collaborative group of co-authors offered reflective support and energy, for which I am deeply appreciative. Opening, healing, and growing together is empowering. This book is 'Our Story', each with our discovered superpowers. I offer my acknowledgment to the readers who consciously step into their own story, now empowered, and I say to you, "You are not alone."

To everyone in my life—friends, family, readers, and fellow seekers—I hold immense gratitude for your presence and support. We are all part of a collective journey, expanding our consciousness and transforming the world.

To the Water, which fills my moments with energy and inspiration, I thank you. You make me feel alive in our remembrance.

. . .

OLGA **DEWAR**

We started as friends and became lovers. We started as lovers and became parents. Our journey together was short but impactful. Thank you for being you: my friend, my lover, my husband, my supporter, my teacher, and father to our amazing son. Without you, I would not be who I am today.

Your life started unknowingly. Your arrival was a great relief. Your childhood was full of constant, unexpected, and turbulent changes. You did not have it easy growing up. I am so grateful for you choosing me to be your mom. I am superbly grateful for your patience, understanding, lessons, authenticity, and love. We've come so far. We are only just beginning to grow our love and support for each other to the highest level.

With love and gratitude,
Your Joy Aficionada
and Amazon Bestselling Author

. . •

LAUREN **BACA**

To my baby sister and sibling for teaching me what true love is and for wanting to make another proud. Twenty-one years ago you shifted my mindset to think beyond myself and while we didn't grow up together as young children, I have grown up so much with you as an adult and watching you both grow into amazing people!

To Bub and Baby Girl, you are my heart and soul! You will always be my fairytale, my happily ever after. I pray that we are always close and I make you proud. I won't always get it right, but I promise to always do my best, and do my best for you!

My hope for all of you is that my life lessons will continue to show you to always bet on yourself and that you have the power to choose, to make changes! Mistakes, life lessons; both good and bad happen, it's all how you pick yourself up and move forward. Never dull your sparkle, edge, and drive. All you need lies within.

ACKNOWLEDGMENTS

To my mom, the fiercest warrior queen I've ever known and the epitome of strength and resilience. Thank you for helping to shape the woman and mother I am today. Thank you, for always cheering me on, pushing me to my limits and beyond, and making me see that I am stronger than I (sometimes) feel.

To my besties who span the country far and wide! Through motherhood, adulting, marriage and divorce—Thank you for continuously being by my side through all of life's beautiful, messy and sometimes chaotic moments. You have all given me so much strength, courage and hope in some of my darkest moments. Thank you for your endless grace, being real, raw and relentlessly by my side, and always keeping me laughing.

Lastly, to my publisher—Thank you for making me see this chapter through! I was hesitant to share my story with the world. But you were right... so much healing came in the making of this chapter.

. . .

KATHRYN **BISLAND**

Scarlett, you saved my life—literally. Your soul calling to me from the other side not only woke me up to what I was unconsciously accepting in my life, but also gave me unwavering courage and certainty that we were going to be together. You are the one who freed me from my unconscious self-imposed chains of lack and imitation, addiction and struggle, and settling for a life that was asking me to give up on myself. It was your voice from beyond, your presence, that quietly guided my every decision and is a gift from God that I am forever grateful for. Your silent strength and joyful focus and perseverance are both traits you have brought into this physical world and it is my privilege and honor to be your guide on this journey of our souls iteration together. Everyday I strive to be the best version of myself to fulfill the role you assigned me—doing right by you to help you fulfill your highest potential, whatever that may be, in the role of your mother. I am so grateful you are my daughter.

Sloane, you taught me that what seems impossible in this physical world can always be transcended, no matter what "they" say. In fact when "they" say I can't or I should just be happy with what I have, I always think of you and the gift you gave me by manifesting in this physical world, against all odds. When I gaze upon your beautiful face and feel your magical soul, it reaffirms that worlds are created from within and if I hold onto my dreams with unwavering faith and peaceful certainty, like I did when you whispered to me "try again" from beyond, that those dreams will come to pass no matter what "they" say. I will spend the rest of my life embodying what I learned from you so that you can grow to become a woman who knows no limits and transcends every obstacle. Even now I marvel at your unwavering clarity & I know as you grow that you'll always have the power to create your deepest desires. Thank you for being my child, my life is better because you are in my physical world.

Matt, you were the missing piece of my puzzle, the person who has always been there but never emerged into the spotlight of my awareness until our girls brought us together through a seemingly impossible and ridiculously unlikely chain of events. There is no denying that we were destined to be together and, while we may have taken our time, we got there in the end and what we have accomplished together has delighted me and brought me back to my true essence and highest potential. Thank you for the way you look at me, for the way you hold the space for all of us to be authentically ourselves, for the way you allow me to be who I really am and wait patiently while I exorcise my demons without judgment. But most importantly, thank you, for loving me and our girls and for being a healed divine masculine—one who loves himself and strives everyday to continually be better than yesterday. Your integrity is an inspiration and it is my honor to run beside you, two free wild horses.

SCAN HERE TO LEARN
MORE ABOUT

www.ingramcontent.com/pod-product-compliance
Lightning Source LLC
Chambersburg PA
CBHW061740120626
46550CB00005B/1843